Interpretationshilfen

Moon Palace

Paul Auster

Cornelsen

Helga Korff

Moon Palace · Interpretationshilfe

Verlagsredaktion
Neil Porter

Umschlagdesign
Klein & Halm Grafikdesign, Berlin

Technische Umsetzung
Antje Kanniga, Berlin

Bilder: S. 5: © Sophie Bassouls/Sygma/Corbis; S. 22 : Cinetext Bildarchiv; S. 26 : John Lund/Getty images ; S. 30 : © Atlantide Phototravel/Corbis, Stefano Amantini; S. 37: © Bettmann/CORBIS; S. 38: © Julie Lemberger/ CORBIS; S. 46: Ullstein bild/Granger Collection; S. 50: © Christie's Images/ CORBIS; S. 63: © Comstock Select/Corbis; S. 73: © Alberto Ruggieri/Illustration; S. 81: © Nik Wheeler/CORBIS

www.cornelsen.de

1. Auflage, 1. Druck 2007

Druck: CS-Druck CornelsenStürtz, Berlin

ISBN 978-3-589-22457-9

Inhalt gedruckt auf säurefreiem Papier aus nachhaltiger Forstwirtschaft.

Contents

All page and line references are to the Cornelsen edition of *Moon Palace* (Berlin: Cornelsen Verlag, 2001); ISBN 978-3-464-37150-3.

Paul Auster

If you look at the early period of Paul Auster's life, you will discover many parallels to the protagonist of *Moon Palace*, Marco Stanley Fogg. They were even born in the same year – 1947.

Auster was born and raised in Newark, New Jersey, just across the Hudson River from New York. His family is Jewish and originally immigrated to the USA from eastern Europe in the 19th century. His father, Samuel Auster, was a landlord who owned several buildings in Newark. His mother, Queenie, was considerably younger than his father. Besides Paul, they had a daughter, who has suffered from psychological problems for much of her life. Auster's parents divorced when he was 17 years old. His father was not at home very often, so he and his son never developed a close relationship. Auster remembers him as a man with a dark, exciting past who was not really present while he was growing up. Auster called his father "a tourist of his own life" and gave the section of *The Invention of Solitude* (1982) in which he writes about his father the title "Portrait of an Invisible Man". His stepfather, Norman Schiff, who his mother married after the divorce and to whom *Moon Palace* is dedicated, seems to have been much more of a father to him, showing interest in his writing career.

Immediately after Auster finished high school, he set off for Europe – all on his own and with very little money – where he spent the summer of 1965. On the trip to Europe Auster started working on two novels, one of which was an earlier version of *Moon Palace*. Upon his return to New York in the fall he attended Columbia University, where he studied English and Comparative Literature. In 1966 he met his girlfriend (and future wife), Lydia Davis, who was also an aspiring writer. Auster received his BA in 1969 and his MA in 1970.

In 1968 protest movements against the war in Vietnam started all over the USA. The campus of Columbia University was the scene of much student political activity. Although Auster did spend a night in jail for participating in student riots, he saw himself as more of a bystander than a political activist, as he always felt himself to be temperamentally unfit for group activities. Like many of his generation, he was critical of American capitalism and especially of the Vietnam policy of the government. He had the good fortune not to serve in the army in Vietnam, because the draft into the army was decided by a form of lottery, and his number was not called.

From 1971 to 1974 Auster spent most of his time in France, working on several literary projects, while earning money through odd jobs. On his return to New York he began to publish some of his early poetry. In 1974 he married Lydia Davis. Their son Daniel was born in 1977, which was a decisive moment in his life, as he saw fatherhood as an experience that separated him from his youth and forced him to become a responsible adult. The marriage to Lydia Davis, however, ended in divorce in 1978.

During these years he became more interested in writing prose than poetry. In 1982 he published *The Invention of Solitude*, but it was with *The New York Trilogy* that he came to public attention. This trilogy consisted of three novels published between 1985 and 1986. His next novel, *In the Country of Last Things* (1987), is memorable for its gloomy and haunting images of life in a futuristic city. In 1989 he published *Moon Palace*. Auster has since then published a novel every two or three years. His main themes are identity, the role of chance and coincidence, of the improbable and the unexpected, as well as what is real and what is imaginary. Some of the characters, like David Zimmer, appear in several of his novels. Auster argues that "Truth is stranger than fiction. What I am after, I suppose, is fiction as strange as the world I live in." (*The Red Notebook*).

Auster has also worked as a screenwriter on several movies: *Smoke* (1995), *Blue in the Face* (1995) and *Lulu on the Bridge* (1998). He has also directed one movie, *The Inner Life of Martin Frost* (2007).

Since 1982 Auster has been married to another writer, Siri Hustvedt, who wrote the widely acclaimed novel *What I Loved* (2003). They have a daughter, Sophie, and live in Brooklyn, New York.

Synopsis

The actual story of Marco Stanley Fogg begins in the summer of 1969. However, before embarking on his story, he looks back at the events in his life that led to this point in time which he considers to be the beginning of his life (cf. p. 7, ll. 14f.).

Marco is an orphan whose mother died in a bus accident when he was 10 years old. She never told him who his father was. He is raised by his Uncle Victor, a clarinetist, who played in several orchestras but ended up selling encyclopedias. He takes him to movies and baseball games, invents stories and fantasy worlds, and explains to Marco all the meanings inherent in his name. During the short period of Victor's marriage, which turns out to be a failure, Marco is sent to a boarding school. Victor sets off on a musical tour of the West with the 'Moon Men' and gives his 76 boxes of 1492 books and his suit to Marco.

Marco starts college at Columbia University in 1965, at first living on campus, then moving into his own apartment on W 112th street. He participates in the student riots on the Columbia campus in 1968. Although quite a drab place, the apartment has the advantage of overlooking the neon sign of the Moon Palace restaurant, which holds a fascination for Marco. The boxes of books first serve as furniture; but when he has to sell the books to get some money, he starts to read all of them one after the other.

The sudden death of Uncle Victor in 1967 leaves Marco devastated, as he is now completely alone. His financial situation is not good and he hardly has enough money to finish college. When he goes to visit David Zimmer, his only friend from college, he finds Zimmer has moved and the old apartment is occupied by some students enjoying a breakfast to which they invite him. Among them is Kitty Wu, a Chinese girl, who calls him her twin brother because they are both wearing the same T-shirt. She feels attracted to him and kisses him good-bye. Alone again, his financial situation worsens; he cuts down on his food and social life, and is finally evicted from his apartment. Too proud to ask his friends for help, and having no motivation to apply for a job, he begins a life in the streets.

The streets of Manhattan fill him with anxiety, so he goes to live in Central Park where people are more tolerant and where he finds a cave to protect him from the weather and criminals. One day he is caught in a heavy rain shower, gets soaked and falls seriously ill. He is found by his friends Zimmer and Kitty, who have been searching for him for days.

Zimmer looks after him in his apartment. Just as his health improves, Marco discovers that he is expected to report for his army physical. His poor health and fragile state as well as his weird monologues save him from military service. He gradually recovers his health, falls in love with Kitty Wu and begins a normal life again.

He then finds a job as a live-in companion for an old man in a wheel-chair. The first encounter with the apparently blind old man Thomas Effing is quite a challenge for Marco, as he turns out to be rude and despotic. Gradually however Marco discovers another side to Effing: as a man of extensive knowledge and education, he teaches Marco how to see and explain things to him, and becomes his spiritual guide and mentor. He also sends him on a journey to the Brooklyn Museum to see the painting 'Moonlight' by Ralph Albert Blakelock. By studying this work of art, Marco is able to understand its message: it commemorates the tranquil and harmonious life of the Indians who, at the time the painting was being created, had become nearly extinguished by the white man. Marco is deeply moved by this discovery and learns more about the unhappy life of the painter, who had been a friend to Effing and who ended up in an asylum.

All these lessons in perception and description turn out to be in preparation for the task Marco is to perform: writing Effing's obituary. Effing begins to tell his true life story to Marco, who is to note down his words and then write three different versions of his obituary. Effing's real name was Julian Barber, he was born in 1885 to a rich man, and wanted to become a painter. He was a great admirer of other painters, but he was also fascinated by the inventor Nikolas Tesla and the new technological advancements at the turn of the 20th century. He discovered that progress is not only a benefit to mankind, as great inventions like electricity can also lead to the electric chair. Disappointed with his marriage and eager to paint the landscape of the American West, he sets off on a journey to Utah, together with a young geologist, Edward Byrne. Byrne dies in an accident and Barber is left alone in the wilderness, about to go crazy with no food and no company, when he comes across a cave, which had been lived in by a murdered man and contains everything that he needs to survive. He discovers that he is able to paint more imaginatively alone in the wilderness than he had been before. From an Indian he learns that the Gresham brothers had killed the man whose body he found in the cave. He expects their return any day. When they do show up, he kills all of them in cold blood and takes their saddlebags full of money. His new life as Thomas Effing in San Francisco starts off in affluence but soon ends in disaster when he is attacked and severely injured, leaving him in a wheelchair for the rest of his life. He goes to Paris in 1920, where he lives for 19 years with the Russian Pavel Shum as his companion and friend. The rest of his life back in New York does not seem to matter for his life story, but he learns that he has a son, Solomon Barber, who he never makes the effort to meet.

Effing sets the date for his own death as 12 May 1970. What remains to be done is to hand out the "stolen" money to anonymous strangers in bills of $50. On one of their last evenings distributing the cash, Effing catches pneumonia in a heavy rain and dies on the day he had predicted. Marco inherits over $7000 and begins a life of great happiness together with Kitty in a loft in Chinatown.

One of the obituaries is sent to Solomon Barber, Effing's son, who contacts Marco in New York. They immediately take a liking to each other. Solomon is an obese man of 350 pounds who is a university teacher. He and Marco become good friends and he moves to New York for a longer stay. He tries to talk Marco into a journey to the West to look for Effing's cave and paintings. Marco and Kitty separate because of a disagreement over whether or not Kitty, who is pregnant, should have an abortion. Marco could not accept the killing of his child, as he sees the child as a chance to experience what it is like to be part of a family. For Kitty, on the other hand, the child is a burden and responsibility she does not want and so she aborts it, thereby losing Marco as well.

Marco then decides to accompany Solomon on the journey to the West. The voyage begins with a stop at the graves of Marco's mother Emily and his Uncle Victor in a cemetery in Chicago. Both Marco and Solomon are overwhelmed with grief and it comes as a shock to Marco when he realizes that Solomon is weeping for the loss of Emily, with whom he had had a brief affair. It becomes clear that Marco was the child born of this affair. Full of anger, Marco hits Solomon, who falls into an open grave breaking his back. In the hospital, father and son tell each other their life stories. Barber tells him that his birth supposedly caused his mother's mental derangement and that he led an isolated childhood due to his obesity. He gives Marco a badly-written novel called “Kepler's Blood”, in which he reveals how he suffered from the absence of his father. He was, however, a gifted student and became a university teacher of History. When teaching at an Ohio college, he had an affair with Emily Fogg, who was one of his students, and was kicked out of the college. He continued his academic life teaching at minor colleges.

When Solomon loses weight in the hospital bed, Marco discovers his own features in his father's face. He has finally come to know who he really is. After Solomon's death Marco continues alone on the journey through the West. He discovers that the area where Effing's cave would have been has been flooded to form a reservoir. Shortly later, his car and money are stolen, and then he walks through California until he reaches the shores of the Pacific Ocean.

Timeline: Moon Palace

Date	Julian Barber/ Thomas Effing	Solomon Barber	Marco Stanley Fogg	other events mentioned in the novel
1883	Birth			
1885				Blakelock paints 'Moonlight'
1893	Sees Tesla at the Columbian Exposition			Columbia Exposition
1905	Death of his father			
1912	Marries Elizabeth Wheeler			
1915			Birth of Uncle Victor	
1916	Leaves for the West, where he almost dies before finding the hermit's cave			
1917	Kills the Gresham Brothers and leaves the cave He is now Thomas Effing	Birth		The U.S.A. enters World War I
1918	Leads a life of debauchery			World War I Armistice
1919	Accident, paralyzed			
1920	Moves to Paris			

Date	J. Barber/ T. Effing	S. Barber	M. S. Fogg	other events
1928			Birth of Emily Fogg	
1932	Meets Pavel Shum			
1934		Writes *Kepler's Blood*		
1936		Attends Columbia University		
1939/ 1940	Moves back to NYC Sees Tesla in Bryant Park	Might have seen Victor at World's Fair Death of Eliza-beth Wheeler		World's Fair in New York World War II Germans occupy Paris
1943		Death of Aunt Clara		
1944		Receives Ph.D. in History		
1945		Teaches at Oldburn College	Victor plays in Cleveland Orchestra	Atomic bombs dropped
1946		Sleeps with Emily Fogg		
1947	Discovers that he has a son	Book on Bishop Berkley published	Birth of Marco Stanley Fogg	
1950			Birth of Kitty Wu	
1953			Victor returns to Chicago	
1955		Book on Roanoke		

1958			Death of Emily Fogg Moves in with Uncle Victor in St. Paul	
1959			They return to Chicago	White Sox lose World series
1961			Dora and Victor get married	
1962 - 1965			Goes to private school	
1963		Book on The American Wilderness		
1964			Dora and Victor divorce Kitty arrives in America Victor and his Moon Men	
1965			Arrives in NYC and lives on campus at Columbia	New York blackout
1966			Moves to own apartment	
1967			Victor dies Experiences financial problems, starts selling books	
1968				Prague spring, Columbia student riots, M.L. King assassinated
1969 July			Sells his last books	Apollo 11 Moon Landing

Date	J. Barber/ T. Effing	S. Barber	M. S. Fogg	other events
1969 August			Meets Kitty Wu at breakfast party	Ticker-tape parade for the astronauts
			Leaves apartment and begins life in Central Park	Woodstock
Sept	Death of Pavel Shum		Moves in with Zimmer	
			Army physical	
Oct			Kitty and Marco become lovers	
Nov	Hires Marco as live-in companion		Starts employment with Effing	Second Moon landing (Apollo 12)
Dec	Starts on obituaries		sees 'Moonlight'	
1970 April	Hands out $ 50 bills to strangers			
May	Death as announced	Receives obituary of his father		
June			Moves to Chinatown loft with Kitty	
Oct		Goes to NYC to meet Marco	Meets Solomon Barber	
1971 Jan		Moves to NYC		
March			Kitty becomes pregnant and has an abortion; Marco leaves her and moves in with Solomon	

July		Travels West to find the cave Falls in the grave in Chicago		Heads West with Solomon
Sept		Dies in hospital		Starts walking after his car and money are stolen
1972				Reaches the Pacific coast
1982				Runs into Zimmer in NYC; plans to write his book

The Story

Chapter One

Summary

What Marco Stanley Fogg calls 'the beginning of my life' (p. 7, ll. 14–15) is the summer of 1969 – the year of the moon landing. In the very first sentences the I-narrator outlines the ups and downs of his unusual life: from financial ruin to his trek across the desert. The reader has been given the outline of his story.

The story in a nutshell

The story actually starts four years earlier, when Marco moves to New York as a first-year student (a freshman) at the prestigious Columbia University. After an obligatory first term in the campus dormitories Marco chooses to move into an apartment in uptown Manhattan. The apartment is on the fifth floor and its windows offer a bleak view, except for the bright neon letters of a Chinese restaurant called "Moon Palace". Marco lives here for the next three years. The neon lights reconcile him with his surroundings and make him think of his beloved Uncle Victor and his band 'Howard's Moon Men'. What also makes him feel at home in this apartment are the boxes of books which his uncle gave him when he went on tour with his band. Lacking any other furniture, he converts the boxes into a table, chairs, a bed, etc., and is pleased with the idea of somehow communicating with these books even if he has not read any of them.

Marco goes to Columbia University.

Marco is a loner and moves into his own apartment.

the Moon Palace restaurant

Uncle Victor's books

The death of his Uncle Victor in the spring of 1967 marks a turning point in his life. Victor had been his only relative and the only person

death of Uncle Victor

to whom he had an emotional attachment after his mother Emily Fogg had been killed in a bus accident in Boston when he was eleven; Marco was never told who his father was. The only link to his past is his name: Fogg had originally been Fogelman (the name of one of his ancestors from Eastern Europe), but on immigrating to America via Ellis Island the name of this ancestor was shortened to Fog which later was to become Fogg. Fogelman derived from the word 'Vogel' and Marco likes the idea of a bird flying all the way across the Atlantic from Europe to America. His other names "Marco" and "Stanley" are associated with two explorers – Marco Polo, who can be said to have discovered China for the Europeans, and Henry Stanley, who explored the central areas of Africa.

death of Marco's mother

Marco and the meanings of his names

Marco's emotional ties to Uncle Victor are very strong. Victor introduces him to baseball, and they both become ardent fans of the Chicago Cubs watching every game in the season. Victor also takes him to the movies a lot. The movie *Around the World in 80 Days* establishes a further connection to the world of exploration and travel, as its hero's name is Phileas Fogg. Victor's fondness for exploring the possible meanings of names and for linking ideas through association, and his creation of imaginary worlds for his young foster child seem to awaken Marco's own fondness for creating roles and poses for himself and for inventing stories.

life with Uncle Victor

baseball

the world of the imagination – storytelling, movies and books

Once a promising clarinetist and member of a world famous orchestra, Victor eventually drops out of the routine of professional life and turns to more casual arrangements with minor bands and to giving music lessons. For a short period he is married to Dora Shamsky, but the marriage fails,

Victor plays in small bands.

Victor and Dora's marriage

among other things because Dora is unable to provide the missing mother-figure for Marco. Marco is sent to a boarding school for three years. After Marco graduates from high school but before he leaves for New York, Victor gives him all his books and a number of odd items, like his tweed suit, which Marco grows very fond of. Victor goes on tour with his band to the West and apart from a few postcards, he and Marco never see each other again. Victor's life as a musician fails and he ends up selling encyclopedias before dying alone in a small town in the West.

Marco is sent to boarding school.

Victor goes on tour to the West.

Life as a college student in the late 1960s was highly political, with protests and demonstrations against the war in Vietnam. Marco and his friend and former roommate David Zimmer get involved in student protests and even get arrested. Marco, however, is not really interested in politics; he is more of a daydreamer caught up in his own problems of self-image. He develops odd character traits and likes to play various roles for his fellow students. Wearing Uncle Victor's suit helps him to separate himself from other students and at the same time to feel strangely connected to and protected by his uncle.

Uncle Victor's suit

As his money finally runs out and all his strategies to cut down on expenses prove futile, Marco decides to sell his books to make ends meet. He decides to read them randomly as he takes them out of the boxes. As his apartment gradually empties, Marco's mind fills itself with all sorts of haunting associations and hallucinations. Yet he manages to achieve some kind of balance for himself, at least for a short time.

Marco's worsening financial situation

Marco sells Victor's books.

With his money running out, Marco reduces his food to the minimum, going hungry most of the time. One day while looking for his friend

Marco experiences hunger.

Zimmer for help, he finds his old apartment occupied by someone else. He is invited in and finds a bunch of young people enjoying what seems – to the hungry Marco – to be an opulent breakfast. Among them is Kitty Wu, a Chinese girl who is immediately attracted to him because he is wearing the same Mets T-shirt as she is. In exchange for the food that these people share with him Marco feels obliged to contribute to their conversation; he offers outlandish stories about voyages to the moon, one being a story by the French author Cyrano de Bergerac, which he claims to be real and not fictitious. Before he leaves the group Kitty Wu tenderly kisses him on the mouth.

Marco meets Kitty Wu.

Marco tells stories about journeys to the moon.

Marco has a last meal at the Chinese restaurant Moon Palace, and the next day – after a discussion about his refusal to find a job to pay the rent – he is kicked out by his landlord. With nothing but Uncle Victor's clarinet case, a small backpack and approximately $30, Marco starts life on the streets.

Marco has to leave his flat.

Commentary

The first chapter introduces us to the childhood and youth of the orphan Marco and gives us an idea of his strange life and behaviour, first as a college student and then as a dropout.

What troubles Marco from the very first line of the novel is the question of **who he really is.** This novel, narrated in the first-person voice, is the long and painful search for an identity, for an understanding of what it means to have a life of one's own. Along the way, Marco will have to discover how much of life is determined by **chance and coincidence**, and how much is shaped by one's own actions and will-power. He

the search for an identity

the role of chance versus self-determination

finds some first hints concerning his identity contained in **his name**: travelling and exploring, but also other meanings resulting from variations on and puns of his name (p. 12, l. 19 – p. 14, l. 12). A particularly meaningful link relates to books and writing, as his initials M.S. (= manuscript) suggest: his life is an unfinished book that needs to be written by himself. It remains to be seen to what degree these associations are relevant or merely games that lead nowhere. Other characters in the novel also have "telling names".

the meaning of names

Another *"link to something larger than myself"* (p. 8, l. 39) is, of course, **Uncle Victor**, but not only in a biological sense as the last remaining relative. Victor's capacity for imagining stories and creating associations affects Marco very deeply and encourages his own gift for imagination and fantasy. Aimlessness and day-dreaming are other characteristics of Uncle Victor, and these may also have influenced Marco's tendency towards idle drifting and refusal to take any action to improve his desolate financial situation. With Uncle Victor gone from his life, Marco is thrown back onto himself and ends up in total despair. Without any larger social network to rely on, he allows his life to be determined by chance and coincidence, and watches himself fall to pieces.

the role of Uncle Victor

It is worth considering whether Uncle Victor is a failure or whether his unusual mind allows him to lead a richer and more unusual life than most other people.

The importance of **books** (besides the fact that we are told that this is a story) is emphasized by the story of the boxes which appear and then gradually disappear from Marco's apartment, thereby undergoing a strange transformation and re-evaluation. Used as pieces of furniture (as bed, chairs, table, etc.), they are a physical support for Marco. The fact that they are books (i.e. a kind of spiritual food) and that they belonged to Uncle Victor make them a mental and emotional

the role of books

support, too. When he decides to sell them, they give him financial support, at least for a while. As Marco reads each one of them before selling them, they also become his spiritual possession. The fact that there are exactly 1492 books in 76 boxes may seem a little too obvious a link between Marco's discovery of himself (his story) and the history and discovery of America. Reading so many books one after the other would probably take more time than is allowed for in the novel. So we discover that the author (or narrator) is probably not taking the number or the reading itself too seriously.

a connection between the USA and Marco (between nationhood and individual identity)

It is also important to note how Marco's apartment transforms as he sells the books. It becomes an empty space in which Marco seems to bury himself as he increasingly becomes cut off from human contact. Marco himself changes in **the empty apartment** – he fills himself up with the contents of the books as he reduces his life to nothing. This foreshadows the experiences which other characters, Effing and Solomon Barber, make in their respective cave and grave.

transformations within closed spaces

Another connection to Uncle Victor is the **tweed suit**, which Marco cherishes and wears until it falls apart. The suit (like the boxes) carries meanings well beyond those of just normal clothes. Neither today nor in the 1960s was it fashionable for a student to walk around in a suit every day, but Marco likes to do things differently and wants to be regarded as different, possibly as a genius impressing others with his intellectual posing (p.22, ll.5–33). Yet there is also a sentimental side to the suit and Marco readily admits to his feelings of comfort and protection when wearing Victor's suit.

Uncle Victor's suit as a coat of identity (even though it is not Marco's own suit or identity)

Another character that Marco relates to is the beautiful **Chinese girl Kitty Wu**. The reader promptly senses that this may be the beginning of a love story that will somehow be continued. The matching T-shirts indicate a tendency in both Kitty and Marco to regard coincidence as a sign of fate or of destiny – as something that has a hidden meaning or message. Another example of establishing correspondences or **associations** is the MOON PALACE neon sign, which Marco immediately interprets as *"a message from the sky itself"* (p. 23, l. 62), making him feel at home. Later, however, when his mind is already dangerously separating from his body, the sign triggers off a whole series of wild associations which eventually give way to mystic revelations.

China plays an important role; here, Kitty Wu and the Moon Palace restaurant.

Everything connects.

The **moon** plays a prominent part in Marco's network of correspondences: while watching the

the role of the moon

moon landing on television he becomes aware of the destructive force with which this act of taking possession is performed (*"planting a flag in the eye of what had once been the goddess of love and lunacy"*, p. 38, ll. 23–24).

The exploration of the moon (and the damage thereby inflicted) will be reflected in the stories of exploration within the novel, which often recount the destruction of the original inhabitants of America by the newly arrived Europeans. The reference to men on the moon also gives a new dimension, allowing events on our planet to be seen from a different perspective (p. 53, ll. 55–56).

The spirit of the 1960s is omnipresent in this first chapter. The many names connected with that period are dropped here simply to evoke this spirit – they are not important in themselves. With the war in Vietnam reaching a sad climax, as far as casualties are concerned, and the protest movement gaining momentum especially on university campuses all over the USA (Columbia University being one of the main battlegrounds), the narrator makes it clear that "*my own story stands in the rubble of those days*" (p. 32, l. 21). Even if he is not a political activist, Marco shares the spirit of critical opposition and resistance to the norm that was prevalent among educated young people in the late 1960s. One reason why he continues at college is that as a student he cannot be drafted into military service (this was called "student deferment"). Another reason is that he wants to keep his promise to Uncle Victor that he would graduate.

the 1960s

What Marco does reject, however, is any kind of official support from the government or other organizations which would involve some commitment on his part. Doing nothing to prevent one's downfall is hard to understand for most readers, but one has to consider that becoming involved with "the system" in any way was considered a form of betrayal. Moreover, by refusing help Marco is forced to rely on himself –

even if this means failure. (This in an odd way reflects the American belief in self-reliance). Part of the intention is also to show that a person must reduce themself to nothing in order to find out who they are.

Revision
(what you learn in this chapter)

- The very first paragraph puts the story in a nutshell: the reader knows what the story is about, so the interest is focussed on the "how".
- Marco is searching for his identity. He does not know who his father is. He looks for meanings within his name. He tries out various roles and likes to create an image of oddness for himself and for others.
- Emphasis is placed on books, on reading, but also on writing (the book of his life).
- His refusal to take up a job is based on his desire to let his life be guided by chance and coincidence.
- The moon offers a kind of spiritual home to Marco, but it also refers to the physical planet about to be explored (and damaged) by man.
- Food and hunger are established as themes of the novel.

Quotes	Analysis
I wanted to live dangerously, to push myself as far as I could go, and then see what happened to me when I got there. (p. 7, ll. 3–4)	For Marco life at this point seems to be an experiment with an uncertain ending.
I was a great one for making up stories back then, and I liked the sound of those sentences, even if they were false. (p. 8, ll. 33–34)	For the narrator storytelling is a pleasure to be enjoyed, and truthfulness is not a value by which stories should be measured.

A bird flying through fog, I used to think, a giant bird flying across the ocean, not stopping until it reached America.
(p. 9, ll. 64–66)

Traveling will become a vital experience for the three main characters of the novel. The tale of immigration is indeed where most Americans begin the story of their American identity.

Given the difficulties that the real world had created for both of us, it probably made sense that we should want to leave it as often as possible.
(p. 12, ll. 16–18)

The imaginary worlds that Victor and Marco love to create in names and stories are an escape from the trouble and complication of the real world.

Chapter Two

Summary

As in the first chapter, the happy outcome of Marco's down-and-out life in Manhattan is given away right at the beginning. His miraculous rescue by Kittty Wu and Zimmer is reconstructed in detail from what Marco himself remembers and what Kitty tells him afterwards.

We are told the outcome of this chapter: Marco's rescue.

Kitty had gone out of her way to find out his address. She had contacted Zimmer and gone to Marco's apartment, but – although she could hear him rambling inside – he wouldn't open the door. When she told Zimmer about his strange behavior, he immediately joined Kitty in her search for Marco. They eventually tracked him down in Central Park.

Kitty contacts Zimmer and they search for Marco.

Marco's odyssey begins with the decision to walk south instead of north in order to avoid meeting friends and acquaintances around the Columbia campus. He is aware of the self-imposed misery of his situation, but is determined to let his steps be guided by chance. He happens to find a

Marco walks around Manhattan.

the $10 bill

ten-dollar bill on the pavement and takes it as a sign that things are going to turn out well. He buys himself an opulent breakfast in a Greek coffee shop and suddenly begins to see the world in brighter colors.

refuge in a movie theater

As the weather becomes unbearably hot in the afternoon he seeks refuge in an air-conditioned movie theater. The audience turns out to be a mixed bunch of dropouts, some of them obviously in the theater for the same reason as Marco: finding a cool shelter and passing the time. The third film in the show turns out to be *Around the World in 80 Days*, which causes him to break down emotionally, as it brings back childhood memories of Uncle Victor. He is so overwhelmed with tears and sorrow that he has to leave the theater.

Marco spends the night in Central Park.

street life versus life in the park

Marco starts to live in the park.

Out on the streets again and with night approaching, Marco now has to consider his options as to how to spend the night. He decides against the sidewalks, the subways and the flophouse, and ends up sleeping behind a bush in Central Park. In the morning he finds himself at the edge of a softball field and is happy to have survived his first night out in the open. In contrast to street life of Manhattan, the Park offers a more tolerant way of life for Marco. He feels that he can blend in more easily with the environment and achieve a kind of inner balance, which sometimes even comes close to happiness. After this he sleeps every night in the park, where he is rarely disturbed or threatened by others, although once an old man does try to steal his clarinet case, which is Marco's most precious possession, as it belonged to Uncle Victor.

Food turns out to be less of a problem as he is sometimes invited to join picnickers or even offered money by strangers. At other times he treats himself to leftovers and, once he has overcome his feelings of disgust and shame, he searches the garbage cans for discarded food. When asked by a suspicious policeman what he was doing he evasively comes up with a story about a sociological study of city garbage cans. Although Marco is aware of the humiliation intrinsic in this kind of life, he tries to explain his situation away as being part of a spiritual exercise or as a political expression of his contempt for the American way of life.

the search for food

inventing stories

Marco is never bored with his life in Central Park. He reads the newspaper every day to keep up with the news in the world and with the fate of his favorite baseball teams, the Chicago Cubs and the New York Mets. He enjoys the nature of the Park, even though it is man-made. He takes part in softball games and talks to strangers. What he is most interested in is watching people and inventing stories about them, some of which he notes down in his notebook.

Marco leads a full life in the park.

Marco observes people.

One night Marco is caught in a heavy downpour and gets soaked through. The next morning he finds a cheap restaurant, orders vegetable soup and tries to dry his hair under a hot-air blower, which turns his hair into a tangled mess. He cuts off all his hair with his last razor, and realizes for the first time how much he has changed and how thin he is – he thinks that he is shrinking and starts worrying that he may soon die. In order to dry his clothes Marco goes to the reading room in the nearby Public Library, but the drying process produces a repugnant smell

Marco gets wet and tries to dry himself.

that disgusts the other people there. Marco is disgusted with himself, too, and leaves.

By now he has a fever and is so weak and ill that he can only just make it back to the Park, where he collapses and throws up. Fortunately he finds a kind of cave among the rocks where he can hide. There he falls asleep, and, when he does wake up again, he starts to hallucinate from the fever. He has wild dreams and visions, one of which concerns the two O's of the Moon Palace sign transformed into two huge eyes, the eyes of God, staring at him. In the end he is able to crawl out and lie on the grass, where Kitty Wu and Zimmer eventually find him. Marco mistakes Kitty for Pocahontas because he had been dreaming of Indians and she is wearing her Navaho headband.

Marco gets a fever and hallucinates.

Kitty Wu and Zimmer find Marco.

Commentary

While the second chapter is not very eventful as far as action is concerned, it does depict the inner struggles within Marco and his constant attempts to rationalize and justify his decision to lead life as a tramp.

The role that **chance and coincidence** play in his life is of utmost importance. Marco tries to turn chance into a kind of philosophy by seeking hidden meanings behind seemingly arbitrary events, like his sudden discovery of a $10 bill. He likes to interpret these events as secret messages to him that confirm that he is on the right track and that all will end well. This philosophy leads him to a basic acceptance of all things that happen to him, a kind of passive drifting along in which he avoids determining himself the course of his life. On the one hand, this leads to an openness and receptiveness for occurrences and happenings

the philosophy of chance

that might otherwise have gone unnoticed. On the other hand, the desire to determine your own life is also quite powerful. Marco tries to solve this paradox by trying not to wish for something in order to get it. "*I began to notice that good things happened to me only when I stopped wishing for them. If that was true, then the reverse was true as well: wishing too much for things would prevent them from happening.*" (p.64, ll.30–33). What for Marco is the happy rescue from an extremely painful and dangerous adventure may seem to the reader a highly improbable and contrived ending of an episode. However, Auster believes that these unexpected things do happen in our lives and that chance and coincidence are part of our reality.

In the first chapter of the novel the reader experiences Marco's life north of Central Park around Columbia University. In this chapter he heads south and experiences a different kind of **New York**. In the streets he encounters the arrogant indifference of passers-by and the rigid control of body language and interaction. Such behavior makes Marco feel very self-conscious, an outsider who does not belong. The high-rise buildings and crowded streets dwarf and shame him. He contrasts life on the streets to life in **Central Park** (cf. p.62, l.9 – p.64, l.3). Here he is able to find the solitude and inner balance he so desperately needs. The Park becomes a sort of home for him. Even when he becomes a little dirtier every day, people do not seem to mind. He says that "*the grass and the trees were democratic*" (p.63, l.50), thus alluding to the ideals of a communal American spirit as reflected in the Declaration of Independence where "Life, Liberty and the Pursuit of Happiness" are constitutionally guaranteed: in the Park you can "*live and let live*"

Civilization can be harsh for the individual.

Nature allows the individual more freedom.

The ideals of the American Constitution can be lived out in nature.

(p.63, l.46), people feed you and may even give you money, and you can even experience moments of happiness (p.64, ll.14–15). This extraordinary power of the Park obviously springs from the wide spaces that allow people to roam freely, but it can also be attributed to **nature**, which, although laid out and designed by man and therefore to a certain degree artificial, has a healing and comforting effect on Marco. He can find privacy and solitude, shelter and human companionship and at the same time allow his individuality to flourish: "*No one blinked if you sat under a tree and did nothing, if you played your clarinet, if you howled at the top of your lungs*" (p.62, ll.39–40). Yet "life in nature" is not only beneficial: it exposes humanity to forces that can also be destructive, e.g. the weather, as we see when Marco almost dies. At this point we see that the love of another human being becomes "*the one thing that can stop a man from falling, the one thing powerful enough to negate the laws of gravity*" (p.56, ll.19–21).

Nature can be harsh; later on, we learn how Effing barely survives in the wilderness.

As in the first chapter Marco is still fond of **playing roles**, of inventing new identities for himself. But now, with his life dangerously close to disaster, the roles he assumes take on a more serious and existential quality. It is not so much

Trying out different roles helps you establish your own identity.

the impression he makes on others that he is concerned with, but the need to disguise his situation – a result of his personal failings. This becomes clear when he says: "*I needed all the props I could find*" (p. 66, ll. 31–32), referring to the use of the toothpick, which he has copied from his knowledge of the picaresque novel *Lazarillo de Tormes*. This disguise gives him the chance to suppress his hunger for a while and to appear to the casual passer-by to be someone who has just had a large meal.

Marco accepts – despite his philosophy of chance – that the life he is leading is a form of failure.

Another role Marco invents for himself is that of observer; this arises from the necessity of reacting quickly when the policeman questions him about his searching for food in garbage cans. The excuse of an urban studies project is certainly a good choice: not only does he get away with it, but observing people and their behavior is indeed one of Marco's main pastimes in the Park.

Marco is an observer of human behavior and life.

As with Marco's empty apartment, another sheltered but **empty space** (here, the cave in the park) becomes the site of a transformation. Marco suffers from fever and starts to hallucinate, imagining the two Os of the Moon Palace sign being the eyes of God. Here, he has reached rock bottom, has been reduced to nothing and is close to death. The cave can also be seen as a symbol of man at his most basic and primitive level.

another transformation within an enclosed space

When he emerges from the cave he dreams of Indians at the time of the arrival of the Europeans and wakes up mistaking Kitty for Pocahontas. This is the first of many references to Indians throughout the novel. Interestingly it is a reversal of something Marco said earlier: "*If Columbus could confuse America with Cathay, who was I to quibble over geography?*" (p. 50, ll. 31–32). Here, Marco has confused a Chinese woman for an

Native Americans, Chinese and Europeans – the formation of an American identity

Indian. The fact that he is dreaming of the first Indian recorded in European history reveals that he has arrived in his homeland America and can start to form his identity.

The question remains as to **what Marco gains from his experiences** in Central Park. Later in life, when he looks back at this time, he realizes that his behavior was foolish: "*it became increasingly difficult for me to make sense of the disaster I had created.*" (p. 78, ll. 16–17) and he apologizes to his friends for having caused them so much trouble. Yet, his intention had been "*to live dangerously, to push myself as far as I could go, and then see what happened to me when I got there.*" (p. 7, ll. 3–4). For Marco this borderline experience is valuable in itself, a venture to the edges of life, even if all he learned is that life is worth living for itself and should not to be thrown away. Another insight is that chance and coincidence are indeed powerful shaping forces in our lives, and that if we allow them to influence our lives, we might discover new territories for ourselves.

A useful experience or a foolish adventure?

Revision
(what you learn in this chapter)

- Marco lets his life be determined by chance and coincidence, thereby hoping to discover some secret meaning to his life.
- His refusal to participate in the American way of life is the political expression of his general decision to let himself be ruled by chance and coincidence.
- Life in Central Park is contrasted with life in the streets of Manhattan: in the streets people are indifferent to others and yet there is a rigid control of behavior; the park offers tolerance and openness for everyone.
- Marco often finds an inner balance in the park, in spite of his frequent mood swings caused by his fragile physical state. He is never bored, he usually finds food, and he experiences moments of happiness.
- To hide his hunger and search for food he invents roles or disguises behind which he can conceal his difficult situation.
- His rescue by Kitty Wu and Zimmer is another example of the power of chance and coincidence, even if it seems rather improbable to the reader.

Quotes and key passages	Analysis
I had jumped off the edge, and then, at the very last moment, something reached out and caught me in midair. That something is what I define as love. (p. 56, ll. 17–19)	Marco's decision to follow his own path lead to disaster. He fails to realize that others around you can help.
p. 62, l. 9 – p. 64, l. 3	The difference between the streets and the park is described. In the streets your appearance is not important but your behavior is. In the park all forms of behavior are tolerated, allowing you to be free and happy.

Once you throw your life to the winds, you will discover things you had never known before, things that cannot be learned under any other circumstances. (p. 64, ll. 17–19)	Marco develops a philosophy of chance, whereby letting go of even your desires brings you things you had not expected.
p. 66, ll. 5–32	Marco indulges in role-playing again, this time to cover up his hunger and need to search for food from garbage cans.

Chapter Three

Summary

Marco recovers slowly from his illness. Zimmer takes care of him and shares the little he himself has with Marco, even letting him sleep in his bed. Zimmer nevertheless makes it very clear that he strongly disapproves of Marco's reckless behavior. Moreover, Zimmer's feelings are hurt because Marco had not asked him – his only friend – for help. Marco is at a loss to explain his behavior, and becomes more and more convinced of his own stupidity and cowardice. Gradually it dawns upon him that he has to change his life completely. He decides to make up for the trouble he has inflicted on others, and become a better and less self-absorbed person.

Zimmer looks after Marco.

Marco then happens to find the draft notice he had placed in the clarinet case the day he left his apartment. The notice informs him that he is to report to the draft board on 16 September – the next day – for his army physical. Failure to turn up would result either in a jail sentence or a large fine. Like many students at the time, Marco has

Marco finds the draft notice.

no intention of joining the army, which would have meant serving in the Vietnam War. The options were either to fail the physical by taking drugs or injuring oneself, to go to prison as a prisoner of conscience or to cross the border illegally to Canada. Due to Marco's state of mind none of these options are really available to him at that moment, and so he goes to the draft-board.

Marco goes to the draft board for his army physical.

Marco is aware of deficiencies in his recollection of what happened at the army board. He remembers the written questionnaire and the physical examination; part of the interview with the psychiatrist is even recorded in detail, word for word. True to his new resolution to no longer lie, Marco answers the questions openly and truthfully, and rambles on to this stranger about his life as if he needed to justify it. Marco tries to convince the psychiatrist of the seriousness of his philosophy concerning the forces of chance. The psychiatrist obviously thinks he is crazy, and Marco is declared 'unfit' for military service.

Marco is not drafted.

Marco discovers that Kitty is in love with him.

With this ordeal over, Marco is now able to pay more attention to what is going on around him. Zimmer points out to him that Kitty Wu is in love with him, but it takes a long argument between the two before Marco is ready to believe him. Zimmer begins to tell Kitty's story, which has parallels to Marco's own story. Kitty was born in Taiwan in 1950. Her family had been opposed to the Communists, and was forced to leave mainland China and live in Taiwan, where they kept a large and luxurious household. At the age of 14 Kitty was sent to a boarding school in America, where she learned to dance and act, among other things. Her parents are now both dead, so – like Marco – she is an orphan and has

Kitty's life story

to fend for herself. She lives off a small inheritance which pays her tuition fees at Juilliard, a famous school for music and dance in New York. Unlike Marco, though, she knows exactly what she wants: to become a dancer. She pursues her goal with great determination.

Marco and Kitty enter into a relationship.

When Marco meets Kitty again he pays a lot of attention to the way she talks and moves, and it does not take them long to fall for each other. Their relationship is very physical, but they have difficulty finding a place for their love-making; Kitty shares a room in a college dormitory with another girl, while Marco is still living with Zimmer and does not want to impose on him, especially since Zimmer's own girlfriend, Anna Blume, seems to have left him (she will in fact become the protagonist of another novel by Paul Auster, *In the Country of Last Things*). So they take every opportunity they can to enjoy their new-found love.

Zimmer gives Marco translation work.

Marco no longer wants to be a burden on Zimmer. It worries Marco increasingly that he is still relying on Zimmer for board and money, so when Zimmer comes home one night and offers him some translation work, Marco jumps at the chance. This will allow him to pay off some of his debt to Zimmer. The translation work gives Marco a chance to find some meaning in his life again.

Marco's friendship with Zimmer

Marco's relationship with Zimmer is not without its own problems. Whereas during their first college year as roommates Marco impressed Zimmer with his eccentricity and ingenuity, it is now Zimmer who seems superior and authoritative. Although he regards Zimmer as a brilliant and thorough scholar, more systematic and insightful than he himself could ever be, Marco's opinion of Zimmer's poems is less favorable. When the translation work is finished, Marco is determined to look for another job and another place to stay.

To celebrate the successful end of the translation work, Marco, Kitty and Zimmer have dinner at the Moon Palace restaurant. At the end of the meal they are given fortune cookies. Marco's reads: "*The sun is the past, the earth is the present and the moon is the future.*" (p. 100, ll. 32–33).

dinner at Moon Palace restaurant: the fortune cookies

Marco starts to look for a job the next morning. At the Columbia student employment office he finds an interesting vacancy as a live-in companion to an elderly man in a wheelchair. He gets the job and is glad to leave Zimmer and live closer to Kitty.

Marco looks for a job.

Commentary

Two other characters in the novel, Zimmer and Kitty Wu, play a larger role in this chapter, an indication that Marco's period of self-centered obsession has come to an end. Marco starts to concern himself with **friendship** (with Zimmer) and **love** (with Kitty). Yet these two characters do

Zimmer and Kitty remain one-dimensional and flat characters.

not really have a life of their own, and do not develop in the course of the novel. In fact, Zimmer only resurfaces once more in the novel in a chance encounter some 13 years later (p. 108, ll. 15ff.).

As for **Kitty Wu**, she is the only female character of importance in the novel. Being Chinese links her to the Chinese restaurant Moon Palace (the sign which had so impressed Marco when he first saw it). Marco calls her "the Dragon lady", as the dragon is the symbol of China. Yet Kitty Wu is firmly embedded in Western (American) culture. In terms of plot development, however, she is the one to push the action forward: she takes the initiative to search for Marco and she kisses him first.

Kitty's story is the first of several "stories-within-a-story" in the novel.

It is worthwhile remembering that when Columbus arrived in America he thought he had reached China.

As a dancer Kitty expresses herself through her body, which is alien to Marco, who is much more concerned with words as a means of expression. He watches her dance performances avidly, paying close attention, but not really understanding them. "*I loved it, but at the same time I did not understand it. Dancing was utterly foreign to me, a thing that stood beyond the grasp of words.*" (p. 100, ll. 10–12). Their relationship is mainly a speechless erotic union of bodies rather than a meeting of minds, although Marco compares Kitty's communicative style to that of a good baseball player (p. 96, l. 29 – p. 97, l. 46) who is able to react sensitively to his partner.

Here, we see that Kitty and Marco are very different people.

A valid question to ask would be why she would fall for someone like Marco – an odd-looking figure, clearly out of step with himself, who devours his food, tells weird and incredible stories, and shows off his bookish knowledge. She calls him *"her brother"* (p. 55, l. 43), implying some form of spiritual connection, but it is likely that she senses that he is someone different and special. For her he is *"Mr. Writer"* (p. 96, l. 19), and she is to become his muse, his source of inspiration and creative power.

David Zimmer is a more literary figure. There are some parallels between Zimmer's life and the early stages of Auster's own career as a writer of essays and poetry. Auster was chiefly concerned with writing poems before he began writing novels, and he also did some translation work as well. Zimmer, however, is more interested in politics: *"rattling on about Trotsky, Mao and the theory of permanent revolution … he resolved the dilemmas of human existence"* (p. 100, ll. 21–27).

Zimmer's concern for his friend is apparent in the way he searches for him and looks after him following the ordeal in Central Park. He admonishes him afterwards in a way that shows not merely deep concern for Marco, but what he expects from a friendship. He offers Marco work and informs him of Kitty's feelings for him (as Marco seems blind to them). Yet eventually Marco wants to leave Zimmer's apartment; living together in the small apartment becomes a burden and because Zimmer's air of superiority bothers Marco. Friendship is shown to have good and bad elements. Despite the bond of friendship that has existed between them, they lose contact with each other as soon as Marco leaves Zimmer's apartment.

Zimmer's caring attitude is reflected later when Barber looks after Marco.

Friendship is never really an altruistic affair.

The amount of space in this chapter devoted to the army physical indicates the significance the author finds in this particular procedure which became a fact of life for young men in the late 1960s during the peak years of the Vietnam War. His account of ways to flunk the physical or to avoid the draft altogether is fairly accurate, and conveys an idea of the options facing many young men at the time. Interestingly he begins his account by saying "*Much of what followed is lost on me now. Bits and pieces remain, but nothing that adds up to a full-fledged memory*" (p.81, ll.55–56). Yet what he does describe is amazingly detailed, especially the conversation with the psychiatrist. The interview is recounted to us in direct speech, and in summary, and is also commented on. This conversation gives us an insight into Marco's behavior. The questions the doctors ask him are basically those which we, as readers, have asked ourselves: "*You don't have a job? … Have you been looking for one? ... You'll have to explain that to me.*" (p.84, ll.18–22). Marco's reasoning is personal and philosophical rather than political. The doctor does not really understand what Marco is trying to say. It is ironic that Marco's failure in Central Park in his quest for "*some secret harmony … some form or pattern that would help me to penetrate myself*" (p.85, ll.47–48) eventually becomes his salvation, as he is not drafted into the army to fight in Vietnam.

Here, Marco's own story is linked to that of the USA. He is part of the larger collective experience of an ongoing war and its consequences.

Auster plays with narrative possibilities (just as he does when he allows Zimmer to recount Kitty's story) by presenting Marco's experience in a selective and fragmentary account.

Looking at the chapter as a whole we can see how Marco's struggle to come to terms with himself, to proceed with his quest for identity, has gained a new dimension: he now knows that "*throwing one's life to the winds*" or "*jumping off the edge*" ultimately leads to disaster and not to a revelation of "*secret harmony*". Yet he has been confirmed in his belief that chance and coincidence are vital forces in determining one's existence. He has also been shown the power of friendship and love.

Revision
(what you learn in this chapter)

- Marco understands that his Central Park experience has been a personal disaster, that he has behaved stupidly and that he has caused others to worry.
- The draft notice and the ensuing army physical are a new challenge to Marco, but his honesty and openness in answering their questions allow him to escape being drafted.
- Kitty and Zimmer both help Marco to regain confidence in himself: Kitty as a lover opening up a new world of tender feelings in him, and Zimmer as an intellectual who stimulates his interest in writing and translating.
- In spite of some common literary interests, Zimmer is a kind of counter-image to Marco, not only in his literary work (poetry) but also in the determined and systematic way he goes about things.
- Kitty establishes another link to China for Marco. She is to become Marco's muse.

Quotes and key passages	Analysis
"Doctor," I said, "do I look like someone who can go without eating breakfast?" (p. 83, ll. 40–41)	Marco sticks to his resolution to give only honest answers. Yet he has not lost his sense of humor.
I thought that by abandoning myself to the chaos of the world, the world might ultimately reveal some secret harmony to me, some form or pattern that would help me to penetrate myself. (p. 85, ll. 46–48)	This is a summary of his philosophy of life which led to him living in Central Park. From now on, he lives more carefully, aware of the dangers inherent in this philosophy.

Much of what followed is lost to me now. Bits and pieces remain, but nothing that adds up to a full-fledged memory, nothing that I can talk about with any conviction. (p.81, ll.55–57)	Memory does not work in a chronological order but selects random fragments from our experience and shapes them into a new system of images independent of our conscious minds.
Kitty had a natural talent for drawing people out of themselves, and it was easy to fall in with her, to feel comfortable in her presence. (p.96, ll.27–29)	Marco admires her intuitive powers to make people talk without feeling ill at ease. It is exactly this quality which later encourages his literary work.
My job was to take a hammer and smash stones into smaller stones, and once those stones had been smashed, to smash them into even smaller stones. (p.95, ll.45-47)	Marco refers to the translation work he has to do for Zimmer. He has always enjoyed working with words and he takes up this challenge as a kind of atonement for his earlier failures.
p.96, l.27 – p.97, l.46	Marco here uses an extended metaphor, comparing a good conversation to the throwing and pitching of a baseball. Marco is beginning to focus on other people again after his long period of obsession and self-pity.

Chapter Four

Summary

On 1 November Marco has his interview with Thomas Effing, an 86-year-old man in a wheelchair. Effing appears to be very frail and blind. But when he talks his voice is vigorous and energetic to the point of intimidating Marco.

Thomas Effing

his appearance

When he starts questioning Marco about his name and views, he becomes even more intimidating. Effing is obviously trying to confuse and irritate Marco, thereby testing Marco's ability to put up with his infirmities and moods, and also to see if Marco is the right person to face the tasks he has ahead for him. Effing seems happy enough with Marco, who moves into Effing's apartment the next morning.

Despite Effing's gruffness, Marco soon gets to know another side of him: he is a widely read and knowledgeable man. He wants Marco to read too – not only aloud to him, but also for himself. From time to time Effing presents him with a selection of books he has to read. They are mostly travel books, dealing with the exploration of unknown territories. Marco is at a loss to know why these books have been selected, and Effing likes to keep him in the dark about his plans and projects. He also likes to play tricks on Marco and make fun of him. When Marco admires his extraordinary memory as to where his books are, Effing replies: "*Stop and think about it. Maybe I creep out here at night and rearrange them while you're asleep. Or maybe I move the books by telepathy when your back is turned.*" (p. 114, ll. 3–6). The important message Effing wants to give here is: "*never take anything for granted*" (p. 114, ll. 8–9).

his knowledge

One particularly disgusting aspect of living with Effing is his manner of eating. The way he eats his soup, and the noises he produces, are so unpleasant that Marco comes to loathe mealtimes. Later on, Marco discovers that Effing does it on purpose, and that he can eat perfectly well in the company of others. He behaves unpleasantly towards his housekeeper Mrs. Hume, who he often accuses of trying to poison him, but she

his manner of eating

knows how to deal with him, having worked for him for nine years. Mrs. Hume is a great support for Marco as she knows how to cope with Effing's mood swings and rudeness, and his despotic and unpredictable behavior. She herself hardly has a life of her own; her only living relative is her brother, a mentally disabled World War Two veteran, who she regularly visits in hospital.

Mrs. Hume

Behind the facade of "the monster", however, there is also a sentimental trait in Effing, which becomes visible when Marco tells him about the early death of his mother. This story of the traffic accident reminds Effing of the death of his companion Pavel Shum, a Russian who had worked for Effing since his time in Paris back in the 1930s and who was run over by a New York cab only a few months before. Marco is given Pavel Shum's coat, and he wears it just as he previously wore Uncle Victor's suit. Effing never fails to make unfavorable comparisons between Marco and Pavel Shum, who was supposedly a master of "*the poetic phrase, a peerless inventor of apt and stunning images, a stylist whose words could miraculously reveal the palpable truth of objects*" (p.123, ll.57–59). Marco often feels miserable living with the constant unpleasantness of Effing and even threatens to leave.

Effing's kindness

Pavel Shum

On their daily walks through the streets of Manhattan Marco is given the challenging task of describing the visible world to Effing, and it is during these walks that Effing becomes his real master. The blind man teaches him to see, to open his eyes to the world – an old literary *topos* found, for example, in the character of Tiresias from Ancient Greek literature and the blind master of Lazarillo de Tormes. Effing teaches Marco to make things stand out by emphasizing their

Marco's task of describing the visible world to Effing

differences instead of their similarities, to look behind the surface of things and then find the words and sentences that would *"separate the extraneous from the essential"* (p.125, ll.56–57). Marco comes to regard this task as a moral activity for his own spiritual advancement, and he practices describing things even when he is alone. His skill in describing improves, so that even Effing approves of his efforts. Marco still does not know what purpose these exercises in the use of language really serve.

From travel books they then switch to reading newspapers, which also includes the reading of the obituaries. It slowly becomes clear that Effing wants Marco to write his own obituary, as he believes his death is near. Effing tells Marco that his own obituary had actually been published 52 years beforehand, when he was believed to be dead. At this point the story of Julian Barber begins, another story-within-the-story, the longest of all these stories in *Moon Palace*.

Effing's obituary

Effing had not always been a cripple. He was born Julian Barber, the son of a wealthy family with a summer house in Long Island. It was here that he became acquainted with the painter Ralph Albert Blakelock, who he considers to be the greatest landscape painter of his time. Blakelock's life story is a sad one: a great artist who ended his days as a mentally deranged penniless man. In his earlier years he had traveled widely in the West and had lived among the Indians for a while, painting all the time. His paintings sold for high prices for the time. Effing is annoyed that Marco has never heard of Blakelock, and sends him to the Brooklyn Museum with precise directions how to get there and instructions to keep his eyes shut for the whole trip to prepare him for

his previous life as Julian Barber

Ralph Albert Blakelock

viewing "Moonlight", Blakelock's most famous painting.

Marco's goes to see "Moonlight".

Marco does exactly as he is told, but when he stands in front of the painting, he is at first disappointed by its size and unspectacular theme, "*a deeply contemplative work, a landscape of inwardness and calm*" (p. 139, ll. 47–48). Only when he takes a closer look at the subject matter – the Indian campfire and the moon – and the unrealistic colors does he begin to understand the nostalgic message of the painting: "*a death song for a vanished world*" (p. 141, ll. 47–48).

Nikola Tesla and electricity

Without any further mention of Blakelock, Effing begins his life story with the story of another man, Nikola Tesla. Like Blakelock, Tesla was a genius but ultimately a failure. As a young

Tesla in front of one of his generators

man, Julian Barber came to admire Tesla's electric inventions – alternating current, the Egg of Columbus, rotating magnetic fields, etc. – and he gives an account of Tesla's battles with Edison and Westinghouse, which Tesla eventually lost. When Tesla built his laboratory, Wardenclyffe Towers, in the town of Shoreham, where Barber lived, the two men happened to meet. Barber is overwhelmed by his presence: "*When Tesla's eyes went through me, I experienced my first taste of death.*" (p. 148, ll. 5–6). When Barber meets Tesla again some 30 years later, he encounters a broken-down old man who talks to birds.

Barber becomes an artist.

Barber has always been interested in art. When his father, a financial tycoon, dies, Julian inherits a vast fortune and becomes "a millionaire artist", free to pursue his artistic goals.

Thomas Moran

The painter Thomas Moran is another of Barber's idols, and it was he who encouraged Barber to become a painter. Moran is the exact opposite of Blakelock. He was the official painter on several expeditions to the West, and his paintings were exhibited in the Capitol building. As Barber sees it, Moran's paintings associate the West with the idea of grandeur, progress and profit. Barber's paintings apparently differ from Moran's in their emphasis on color and light. With his passion for landscape he decides to go out West himself and paint what he sees there. The project involves another participant, Edward Bryne, a young geologist and topographer, equally eager to map out the West.

Barber decides to head out West.

Barber's unhappy marriage

The other reason which encourages Barber to leave is his wife, Elizabeth Wheeler. Their marriage has been a failure from the start, as she does not enjoy the sexual side of marriage. Yet, anxious about her husband leaving, she offers herself to him for the last time (which is to have consequences of which Barber is unaware for a long time).

Barber and Bryne go on horseback to the Great Salt Desert, where Barber paints passionately. When they move on, their guide Scoresby leads them into a dangerous area in the mountains. Bryne's horse loses its footing and falls down the rocky slope, leaving Bryne seriously injured. The guide abandons them and Bryne dies three days later. Now Barber is completely alone with no hope of survival and believes he is about to go crazy.

Barber in the West

Commentary

This chapter and the next are the longest in the novel and contain what may be called "the Effing/Barber story". The fourth chapter sits right in the middle of the odd number of seven chapters, with the description of Blakelock's painting in the very center of the book.

In this chapter the perspective changes from Marco to Effing.

As a companion, Effing is a nightmare: his eating habits are revolting, and his rudeness and unpredictable temper are a severe trial to Marco's patience and good will. It is hard to tell when Effing is lying or telling the truth, but there always seems to be a secret plan or deliberate intention behind his behavior. He plays a game of confusion and deceit with Marco, with the aim of teaching him to look behind the surface of things and never to take anything for granted. Marco is eager to learn from his "*self-appointed mentor to my inner progress*" (p. 110, l. 38), as he calls him, and eventually comes to appreciate Effing's qualities of critical insight and his knowledge of the world. There are three things that Marco learns from his master:

Effing is Marco's mentor.

what Marco learns from Effing

1. He learns to distinguish between the essential and the unimportant, to question the obvious, and to see beyond the surface of things.
2. He learns to use words to create images in the mind of visible objects, thereby "making things stand out".
3. He learns to view the world with skepticism, to question the value of progress and technological advancement, and to understand the failures of the past.

The process of bringing the world into the mind of the listener (or reader for that matter) through words is of special importance here, because Marco will himself become a writer. Reflections on the writing process are a major characteristic of postmodern literature. Marco is made aware that literary creation is not a straightforward affair: "*one meets with failure too often to exult in the occasional success*" (p. 126, ll. 2–3). For a writer it is important to realize that words themselves are arbitrary, whereas the objects around us are unique. Both language and visual perception are unreliable, as we can be deceived by both words and by images. They do not offer any certainty or general truth. The only thing one can hope for is to allow the listener/reader "*to feel his own mind traveling toward the thing*" and "*to do the crucial work on his own*" (p. 125, ll. 58–60). The literary process itself is, firstly, one of viewing and distinguishing and, secondly, one of simplifying and reducing in order to achieve the construction of "*an image on the basis of a few hints*" (p. 125, l. 59). This is why in all great literature there are rarely in-depth descriptions of objects, but "hints" to allow the reader to form their own impression. By learning this, Marco becomes more humble and patient when faced with the difficult task of

the importance of using words well

describing the world to a blind man, but he never gives up. Inadequacies, errors and failure are part of the path that leads to a form of success.

A number of landscape painters are mentioned in this chapter, each of them presenting different visions of the West. The American West in the 19th century was a largely unexplored and unmapped area in the newly-formed USA. It attracted explorers, pioneers, settlers, speculators

the role of landscape painting in presenting an image of the West

John Gast's "American Progress" illustrates the westward movement of progress.

and artists, each of whom had their own dreams, hopes and plans for the area. Their reports, descriptions, maps and pictures created an image of the West that did not necessarily give "the true picture". The West first came to the attention of the wider American public through the paintings and reports of these early explorers. By choosing two very different types of painters such as Moran and Blakelock – each of whom Effing admires for different reasons – the reader is shown the wide range of possibilities of viewing the West. The painter as explorer is the role which Effing attributes to Moran. In many paintings (though not by Moran) from the decades between 1850 and 1890 the clash between civilization and nature, the line between cultivated land and wilderness is made visible by a diagonal line separating two areas of dark and light. (You can find some of these paintings at www.learnetix.de/moonpalace • Chapter Four • Manifest Destiny in Art). The painter, who is sometimes present in these pictures, is the one who, by painting the wilderness, also destroys its "untouched virginity". He becomes the accomplice of the explorer and pioneer, who prepare the land for cultivation. Blakelock, on the other hand, is the conscience and guardian of what has gone. Whereas Moran is concerned with the future, Blakelock's interest lies in the past. Blakelock traveled alone, "*wandering through the wilderness for weeks on end, never seeing a soul*" (p. 133, ll. 60–61), whereas Moran went with official expeditions. With his "*memorial for a vanished world*" Blakelock is drawing attention to the lost harmony of the world of the Indians and recalling a romantic vision of the West, which is just as "invented" as that of other artists.

Thomas Moran celebrates the arrival of civilization.

Blakelock looks back to the time when harmony existed between man and nature.

The description of the painting "Moonlight" is set apart from the rest of the novel by its impersonal and nearly scientific style. The smallest details, the technique, the color, as well as the overall impression are captured in the description. It can be considered a showpiece of how Marco has put Effing's lessons into practice. Marco approaches the picture from the surface of the objects presented on the canvas (e.g. commenting on the brushstroke, the use of color,

Marco's description of "Moonlight"

etc.) before considering its message: *"If he hadn't been trying to represent an actual landscape, what had he been up to?"* (p. 140, ll. 22–23). The answers can only be speculations, as we can see by imprecise words and phrases like *"seemed to be saying"*, *"wondered"*, *"to imagine"*, *"perhaps"*, *"only guessing"*. Marco comes to the conclusion that the painting offers a nostalgic view of the harmonious blending of human figures (Indians) with nature. The date of the painting (1885) confirms his suspicion, as at that moment in history the way of life of the Indians was nearing extinction.

Marco's analysis of "Moonlight"

A number of references in this chapter are made to notions of progress and technological advancement. Just as two artists, Moran and Blakelock, are contrasted, so too are two inventors, Thomas Edison and Nikolas Tesla. Tesla is to lose the battle over electricity, although in Effing's eyes he is the more ingenious and brilliant of the two. Effing hails Tesla as *"Mr. Tomorrow, the prophet of a new world"* (p. 150, l. 1) at the height of success. Like Blakelock, however, he ends in poverty, his failure reflecting the end of the dream that progress is always for the best. The ambivalence towards the idea results from the knowledge that technological advances are both good and bad for mankind. Every new invention has its price, and progress contains elements of destruction and annihilation. Effing reveals this in a number of examples:

the role of technological advancement in bringing progress

Geniuses can end up as failures.

Progress can be destructive.

1. Electricity has not only brought light and energy to mankind but also the electric chair and electrocution;
2. Tesla's Wardenclyffe Tower and a number of old mansions on Long Island were replaced by tract houses and traffic facilities (p. 143, ll. 49–51);

3. Westward expansion and the railroad – just like the moon landing – mutilated and destroyed valuable tracts of untouched wilderness and destroyed the lives of the Indians, who lived in harmony with nature.

Effing also attempts to denigrate technology: he claims with great pride to have caused, by the power of telekinesis, the New York blackout of 1965 (p. 107, ll. 43–50). As an act of revenge for his own blindness he wanted the whole city to live in the same state. Effing intends to prove the superiority of will power over the physical world, of mind over matter.

the role of Effing's life story within the novel

The final question to do with this chapter is why the perspective has changed so dramatically from Marco to Effing. While in other chapters we learn about Marco's life, here we learn of the life story of a totally different person. On the one hand, all the major themes and motifs of the novel – such as "progress", "art", "identity", "guilt and atonement" – are related in one way or another to Effing, and through his double identity as Effing and Barber he integrates the various parts and sub-plots within a whole. On the other hand, he provides a link to the past, to the history of the USA as it expanded westward and made enormous advancements in technology, thereby forming a new identity for itself. Inspired by its belief in its God-given path (Manifest Destiny) and by its technological power, the USA invented its own self-image. Until now Marco has situated his identity within his own era, that of the 1960s. In this chapter his identity is put into a larger perspective, a person seeking his identity within the history of a nation in search of its own identity.

Revision
(what you learn in this chapter)

- Effing is a contradictory figure: he can be a vicious monster who intimidates and insults Marco, but he can also show kindness and sympathy.
- Effing is a spiritual mentor to Marco. The blind man teaches Marco to open his eyes to the secrets behind the visible world and instructs him in the use of language.
- Marco's "lessons" are a preparation for writing Effing's obituary.
- The detailed description and analysis of "Moonlight" is a practical application of Effing's teachings.
- Painters have very different views of the West: they can either become accomplices of explorers opening up the wilderness for settlement and civilization or they can deplore its loss.
- Progress and technological advancement are not necessarily good; they also bear the germ of destruction.

Quotes and key passages	Analysis
My name and I have been through a lot together, and I've grown rather fond of it over the years. (p. 104, ll. 17–18)	Faced with Effing's rude criticism, Marco proudly defends his name, which has become an important part of his identity and his only link to his family and his past.
Are you sure you're alive, boy? Maybe you just imagine you are. (p. 107, l. 68)	Effing is confusing Marco on purpose: he wants him to question everything, to never take anything for granted.
The world enters us through our eyes, but we cannot make sense of it until it descends into our mouths. (p. 124, ll. 13–14)	The complex relationship between seeing and speaking, between images, words and meaning is addressed here.

I was no longer able to see them as moons. They became holes in the canvas, apertures of whiteness looking out onto another world. Blakelock's eye, perhaps. A blank circle suspended in space, gazing down at things that were no longer there. (p. 142, ll. 21–24)	After his visit to the Brooklyn Museum, Marco looks at other paintings by Blakelock with similar topics. The moon is seen here as a means to gain a new and wider perspective on our world that encompasses a look backwards in time.
Manifest Destiny! They mapped it out, they made pictures of it, they digested it into the great American profit machine. Those were the last bits of the continent, the blank spaces no one had explored. Now here it was, all laid out on a pretty piece of canvas for everyone to see. The golden spike, driven right through our hearts. (p. 150, ll. 34–39)	The American ideological belief in westward expansion as an expression of God's will lends itself well to profitable land speculation and railroad construction. 'The golden spike' was the last nail, made of pure gold, that was driven into the last sleeper of the two transcontinental railroads meeting at Promontory Point in Utah in 1869.
A man can't know where he is on earth except in relation to the moon or a star. […] A here exists only in relation to a there, not the other way around. (p. 155, ll. 58–63)	The importance of relativity, of determining one's position in relation to another position is illustrated here. The moon can teach us where we are on our planet.

Chapter Five

Summary

The daily routine of Effing narrating the story of his life has been going on for two or three weeks now; Marco has been noting down as much as he can of Effing's original words during their morning sessions. The story now shifts from a first-person to a third-person narrative.

Barber alone in the wilderness

After the death of his companion Byrne, Barber believes that his life has come to an end as well. He only has enough supplies to last for another two days. He decides to move on, even though he has no idea where he is. As he slowly loses his mind, he starts howling and screaming. However, he spots a cave at the top of a cliff. Upon entering it he finds it to be completely furnished and containing food supplies which would last at least for a year. He finds a dead man lying in the bed, obviously shot recently. There are no indications as to who he might be. As the dead man is about the same age and stature as Barber, he immediately decides to take on this man's identity and live in the cave for as long as the supplies would last. He buries the man, puts on his clothes and decides to just pretend to be him should anyone come along.

the cave

Barber's life in the cave

A new life is suddenly offered to him, which he enjoys immensely at first. After some time, however, he begins to feel terribly lonely, and starts to suffer from hallucinations. Slowly he recovers and decides to keep it a secret that he is still alive, so that his family will believe he is dead. What keeps him going at this point is the discipline of a daily routine and stocktaking of his supplies, which he comes to regard as a personal triumph over despair. And then he begins to paint again, which restores his spirits and energy and makes him extremely happy. His supplies of paint and canvas last for two and a half months. He covers 40 canvases with his paintings, and then he paints their backs as well, and after that the furniture and finally the wall of the cave until his paint finally runs out.

Barber starts to paint.

Two things limit his creative production: firstly, he does not have enough materials, a fact that actually increases the intensity of his painting; secondly, the knowledge that no one will ever see his pictures. Instead of despairing over this lack of communication with an audience, he finds that it liberates him: he has no need to pay attention to the criticism and judgments of others. He can also forget about artistic conventions: "*He untaught himself the rules he had learned, trusting in the landscape as an equal partner, voluntarily abandoning his intentions to the assault of chance, of spontaneity, the onrush of brute particulars. He was no longer afraid of the emptiness around him.*" (p.171, ll.49–53). His motifs are landscapes which he paints from nature, trying to put the gigantic spaces and the emptiness around him into color and form.

Once his painting materials have been used up, he turns to writing, keeping one log of his daily activities and another of his thoughts and observations, moving from one form of artistic expression to another, until his notebooks too run out.

Barber keeps journals.

His first visitor appears in March, a big man in odd clothes, whose face is deformed by a scar. Barber discovers that he has nothing to fear from this good-humored but simple-minded man called George Ugly Mouth, and they enjoy an afternoon of smoking and good companionship together. Barber learns that the man whose corpse

George Ugly Mouth turns up.

he found was called Tom, and that he had been involved in the criminal activities of a gang of outlaws called the Gresham brothers, and that the cave was probably intended for use as a kind of hide-out, which would account for the food supplies. The gang had obviously wanted to get rid of Tom and had killed him in cold blood.

Barber learns about the Gresham brothers.

Barber now knows that his period of solitude and creative experimentation will soon come to an end. As he does not want to leave his cave yet, he prepares for the arrival of the Gresham Brothers. He becomes extremely watchful and alert in order not to be taken by surprise. After a month of waiting the Greshams finally arrive. They unsuspectingly go into the cave, eat and get drunk, and when all but one are asleep, Barber goes in and shoots them all.

the gunfight with the Greshams

The next morning he finds the Greshams' saddlebags, which contain $20,000 in cash, some jewelry and another $10,000 in investments. All of it is obviously stolen money, but the idea of returning the money never occurs to Barber. He prepares to leave his cave, stores away the paintings and the notebooks and cleans the place up, not without a trace of regret for leaving behind his shelter, the place which had saved his life and where he had been so happy and creative. He takes the saddlebags and rides off to a new future. He eventually arrives in San Francisco and signs the hotel register with the name "Thomas Effing". Thomas stands for his painter friend Moran, while Effing is another way of saying the swear word "fucking", which seems appropriate for his life so far.

Barber takes the stolen money.

a new identity: Thomas Effing

From here on the narrative takes greater jumps through its chronology, with whole of months and years being summed up in a couple of sentences; some events contradict others and some events take place in the wrong settings. At first Effing lives a life of luxury, having increased his fortune by successful financial dealings. One day he is confronted with a former colleague of his father's who recognizes him as Julian Barber. Effing manages to convince him that he is mistaken, but from then on he withdraws from social life, afraid of having his true identity and guilt revealed. Instead he launches into a life of debauchery in Chinatown, where he seeks oblivion in its opium dens, brothels and gambling rooms.

Effing's life in San Francisco

It is in San Francisco where he meets with the accident that paralyzes him. Walking home one night along one of the city's steep roads, he is hit on the head by a stranger, slides downhill and crashes into a lamppost badly injuring his spine. This accident leaves him paralyzed and in a wheelchair for the rest of his life. Effing comes to see this fate as a form of punishment for his sins, – as he has been punished in this way, he no longer feels the need to punish himself: "*His crime had been paid for, and suddenly he was empty again: no more guilt, no more fears of being caught, no more dread*" (p. 188, ll. 17–20). Nine months later he travels by ship to Paris on a false passport, having put what is left of his money into a Swiss bank account. He continues to live in Paris until 1939, when the war breaks out. The rest of the life is covered by one laconic sentence which Effing dictates to Marco: "*After leaving Europe at the beginning of World War II, Mr. Effing returned to New York, where he spent the last thirty years of his life*" (p. 191, ll. 58–60).

Effing is attacked and paralyzed.

Effing leaves for France.

the rest of Effing's life

A kind of spiritual kinship between Effing and Marco grows during the time that Effing recounts his life story: *"I began to live inside that voice as though it were a room, a windowless room that grew smaller and smaller with each passing day"* (p.184, ll.12–14). Marco no longer wonders about the truth of Effing's narrative, although some of it strikes him as rather improbable and contrived. One reason for this is that Marco himself has lived through similar experiences of loneliness, despair and solitude, and has had his own experience in a sort of cave in Central Park. He can now regard Effing as a "kindred spirit".

It is now his task to write out three different obituaries for Effing:

the three obituaries

1. an obituary for a newspaper, covering only the bare facts (500 words);
2. "The Mysterious Life of Julian Barber" for an art magazine, which is more sentimental in tone (3000 words);
3. "Effing's story as told by himself", an autobiographical story, an edited version of the complete story in 100 pages.

This last version is the one that Marco has to work on most carefully and which Effing is most interested in.

One morning Marco finds three books lying on his bed. They are about early American history and were written by a certain Solomon Barber. Effing tells Marco that Solomon is his son, conceived in 1916 before he left for the West. He had found out about him through Pavel Shum's investigations and had followed his career as a historian teaching in several minor colleges. Apparently he had been kicked out of one college for an affair and his academic career had suffered during the McCarthy era. His mother (Effing's wife) had died in 1939. Effing has never made any effort to meet his son, as he had once promised

Solomon Barber – Effing's son

himself never to make any inquiries into the past once his new identity was established: "*No turning back – that was the important thing. No regrets, no pity, no weak-minded sentiments. By refusing to find out about Elizabeth, I kept myself strong*" (p. 195, ll. 69ff.). He does, however, decide to leave his son all his money after his death, which he says will occur on 12 May – leaving him two more months to live.

Effing distributes his money to strangers.

With his will written and all his affairs taken care of, there remains one last task for Effing: he wants to return the money that he took from the saddlebags of the Gresham brothers. He still feels guilty about the theft and plans to hand out $20,000 in bills of $50 to anonymous strangers in the streets over several weeks. Marco helps him distribute the money to those who seem most deserving. Towards the end they come across a black man called Orlando who invites them to walk under his umbrella, which consists only of spokes, to keep out of the imaginary rain. Both Marco and Effing are so fascinated by this show that they heartily play along. Orlando's last sentence to them seems to foreshadow future events: "*If you're not ready for everything, you're not ready for anything*" (p. 209, l. 60).

Orlando and his umbrella

Effing's end is now approaching rapidly. He catches pneumonia on the very last day of distributing the money, when he deliberately allows himself to get wet in the rain. He spends his last days in bed with Marco sitting by his side. He dies two minutes after midnight on 12 May, his prediction was correct. Effing has masterminded his own death. Effing's ashes are strewn over the waters of New York harbor. When Mrs. Hume hands Marco a brown bag as a last gift

Effing's death

Effing leaves Marco some money.

from Effing, he discovers that Effing has left him more than $7,000.

Commentary

In this chapter various narrative modes are used. The second part of Effing's life story differs from the first not only in its narrative perspective but also in style: whereas Effing's story in Chapter Four had been narrated in direct speech, bearing all the marks of spontaneous rhetoric such as exclamations, unfinished sentences, swear words and jumps from one event to another, in Chapter Five the shift to a third-person narrator (Marco) and reported speech produces a more elaborate and refined version of Effing's story. It follows a chronological pattern and on the whole gives a less subjective view of what happened.

One of the main interests in this chapter is Auster's use of different narrative modes.

It is no longer important whether the story (or certain episodes) is true or a lie, or whether Effing has remembered it correctly; what matters is "the inner meaning", which can be conveyed just as well by "*inventing a parable*" (p. 183, l. 54). This change in narrative mode appears exactly at the moment that Julian Barber is "extinguished" and a new identity is about to be formed. By addressing him as "Tom", George Ugly Mouth has laid the basis for this transformation, and Barber can slip into the identity of the hermit. Barber says "*because it was inconceivable to him [George Ugly Mouth] that a man who answered to the name of Tom could be anyone other than the Tom he was looking for, he had hastily altered the facts to match his expectations, justifying any discrepancies between the two Toms as a product of his own faulty memory*" (p. 174, ll. 34–39), thereby indicating that the power of imagination can often be stronger than physical evidence. Effing keeps up the role of the hermit only as long

The change in narrative mode occurs when Barber changes identity.

as it is useful; when he gets to San Francisco he becomes "Thomas Effing", an identity he keeps for the rest of his life until he reveals his past to Marco.

Quite a different type of narrative mode is used in the episode of the Gresham brothers. This incident is set apart in style and theme from the rest of Effing's story. It follows the pattern of the Western genre, familiar from popular literature and the movies: a group of gangsters is caught in a fight with an individual who defends what he considers to be his property (= the cave) and life; the bad guys are killed in a tense shoot-out and the hero survives and gets the other men's property. The conventional props consist of bullets and rifles, horses, whiskey, a card-game, a shoot-out, and a large sum of (stolen) money in saddlebags. Why is a stereotypical scene from pulp fiction included in a literary text dealing with questions of identity, and the perception of truth and beauty? The episode forms a part of a whole; the novel consists of various modes of narration coexisting side by side. Auster wants to obliterate the line between "high" and "low" literature, as he views each form as being equally valid, judged by the degree to which it fulfills its function within its own context and within the whole. Just as is the case with the various painters' interpretations

The Western episode stretches the credulity of the reader, as Barber acts like a skilful gunman rather than a painter from the East.

In post-modern literature all genres are considered equally valid.

of the West, the Western genre adds yet another image of the West to the novel.

The obituaries are another example of different modes of "stories" being placed side by side. They differ in length and tone, but contain the same "story". Auster is pointing out that there is no "real" or authentic story, just as there can be no single one authentic narrative of a life. Effing's life has been a series of self-inventions and re-constructions of identity, so an adequate reflection of it is to sum it up in three differing versions. In Marco, Effing finds a congenial author, a kindred spirit, who responds to his unusual story in an understanding way. Marco discovers parallels to his own story, e.g. the experience of finding protection in a sheltered place (the cave), the experience of living through periods of extreme despair and fear of death. They also share a concern for the truthful expression of the visible world, whether in images or in words. Marco struggles to find adequate language to express "the essence" of things around him, just as Effing tried to do the same with his landscape paintings, in which he transformed the "emptiness" of the landscape around him into art.

Marco and Effing share similar experiences.

The topics of **guilt and redemption** or **crime and punishment** have been only slightly touched upon so far (e.g. Marco's feelings of guilt about his irresponsible behavior when he ran out of money). Towards the end of his life Effing feels guilt for various reasons and believes that he has to make amends for some of the wrongs he has done to others.

He feels that at least after his death his son Solomon has a *"right to know about his own past"* (p. 197, l. 68) and should have an idea of who his father really was. This is to make up for the fact

This also reflects on Marco's story, as he too does not know who his father is.

that he never met him, even after having become aware of his existence. Effing acknowledges his fatherhood, and leaves most of his money to Solomon. Marco is to send him the long version of the obituary. Probably the best legacy Effing makes is one which neither he nor Marco is aware of at the time: through the connection Marco establishes with Solomon, the latter will finally be able to become a father himself and come to realize that Marco is his son.

Effing may see the distribution of the $20,000 as part of his atonement, but as it has little effect on Effing, who seems to enjoy the activity, one cannot really talk of "punishment".

The description of the accident in San Francisco as a form of punishment is also not unproblematic. Effing never learns who attacked him or why. This allows him to interpret his injury "*as a form of cosmic retribution*" (p. 188, l. 24) for his actions.

Effing's "crimes" have always sprung from his egotism. He has a nasty streak that allows him to be rude and hurtful to others: he treats Marco and Mrs. Hume badly, he leaves his wife, he never allows his son to know his father, he kills men with whom he has no quarrel in cold blood, and he lives off stolen money. But he does have a sense of responsibility in a larger sense: he teaches Marco to see beyond the surface of things (and his harsh manner is effective in doing this) and to have a better understanding of the nation from which he comes.

"*Mind over matter*" (p. 212, l. 31) is the essence of Effing's philosophy of life. The only time when Effing does show the power of his will is when he fixes the date of his own death. However, we may question to what extent Effing has not actually pushed matters by exposing himself to the rain and refusing any protection.

His claim to have caused the New York blackout (p. 107, ll. 43–50) through telekinesis is not at all credible, but one may ask whether this is not some form of joke. Yet Effing's admiration for Orlando, the black man who claims to be protected from the imaginary rain with his useless umbrella, shows how he (like Marco) is prepared to allow the world of the imagination to become real for him. "*If you're not ready for everything, you're not ready for anything*" (p. 209, l. 60).

While Effing's claims are often untruthful, it is worth remembering that Marco's story is also a fictional piece of work. What is important is the story.

Effing's insistence on the power of the will and on being able determining one's fate differs from Marco's own philosophy of chance and coincidence.

Revision
(what you learn in this chapter)

- Auster plays with narrative modes: the shift from first-person direct speech in Chapter Four to third-person reported speech in this chapter corresponds to a change of identity – from Julian Barber to Thomas Effing. The use of the Western genre in the Gresham episode creates another image of the West (which is just as valid as the images created by the painters). Three different versions of the obituary show that the life of a person can be viewed from different yet equally valid perspectives.
- Effing produces painted landscapes without the constraints of rules or public judgement; his only limitations are his lack of materials.
- Marco feels some kind of spiritual kinship with Effing: he sees parallels to his own story and is not put off by the improbabilities contained within Effing's story.
- Effing believes in the power of mind over matter. Only in death does he really achieve this. This philosophy contrasts strongly with Marco's belief in allowing chance to decide the course of one's life.

Quotes	Analysis
When a man feels he has come to the end of his rope, it is perfectly natural that he should want to scream. (p. 166, ll. 23–24)	The experience of his companion's death and the utter hopelessness of his situation in the canyon make Effing howl and scream, just like Marco had done towards the end of his stay in the cave in the park.
The true purpose of art was not to create beautiful objects, he discovered. It was a method of understanding, a way of penetrating the world and finding one's place in it. (p. 171, ll. 44–47)	Similar to Marco's process of putting the visible world into words and images, Barber tries to get at the essence of things and establish an artistic relationship to them.
The hermit's cave, the saddlebags of money, the Wild West shootout – it was all so farfetched, and yet the very outrageousness of the story was probably its most convincing element. It did not seem possible that anyone could have made it up. (p. 183, ll. 55–58)	The reader is not as easily convinced of the truthfulness of the story as Marco, but goes along with it as it offers comic relief from the earlier passages of traumatic experience and despair.
My own story is just as preposterous as Effing's, but I knew if I ever chose to tell it to him, he would have believed every word I said. (p. 183, l. 67 – p. 184, l. 2)	Marco discovers a kindred spirit in Effing and feels close to him, although neither of them is in the least aware of the true relationship between them (grandfather and grandson).

Everyone has a right to know about his past. I can't do much for him, but at least I can do that. (p. 197, ll. 67–68)	Effing wants to make up to his son Solomon Barber for having denied him a father. Maybe Effing addresses Marco's fatherless fate here as well: when Marco had told him about his childhood he had shown sympathy and feeling for the first time.
This was imagination in its purest form: the act of bringing non-existent things to life, of persuading others to accept a world that was not really there. (p. 209, ll. 42–44)	Orlando with his broken umbrella creates a reality that goes beyond that of tangible visible matters, merely by the power of suggestion and imagination.
You're a dreamer, boy. Your mind is on the moon, and from the looks of things, it's never going to be anywhere else. You have no ambitions, you don't give a damn about money, and you're too much of a philosopher to have any feeling for art. What am I going to do with you? (p. 215, ll. 66–70)	Before he dies Effing worries about Marco's future. He has recognized Marco's penchant for drifting and introspective reflection, and wants to warn him.

Chapter Six

Summary

Marco and Kitty live in Chinatown.

Financially independent and living together with Kitty Wu in a spacious loft in Chinatown, Marco experiences a period of extreme happiness. A new life begins for Marco, as he and Kitty create "a home". They furnish the loft with very few necessary objects; Kitty uses the space for her dancing practice. During her summer vacation

Kitty works for a trade magazine, while Marco spends his time doing the house work, writing various texts and articles, and reading some of the authors Effing used to talk about. Although Chinatown remains foreign territory for Marco, as he can neither communicate with the inhabitants nor understand their way of life, he enjoys the unfamiliar life in his new surroundings as if he were living in another part of the world.

Sending the two shorter versions of Effing's obituary to the *Times* and an art magazine does not have any results: the *Times* never responds and the art magazine wants more evidence concerning the biography of Julian Barber and the quality of his paintings which, of course, Marco cannot provide. The longest obituary is sent to Solomon Barber, who replies warmly and announces his upcoming visit to New York. Barber suspects from the very first moment of their encounter that he might be Marco's father, but he doesn't tell him so. Their first meeting is quite surprising: Barber is a very large fat man, and Marco is a little bit surprised by his appearance, but he is immediately won over by Barber's friendliness. Barber says he knew a student called Fogg, who turns out to have been Emily Fogg, Marco's mother. At this point we learn of Solomon Barber's life, which he only tells much later when he is near death. He had a love affair with Emily Fogg while teaching at a college, for which he was promptly dismissed. Barber tried in vain to contact Emily afterwards, but she refused to talk to him again. Barber's later attempts to contact Uncle Victor were also unsuccessful. Uncle Victor refused to respond to his repeated calls because he was afraid of losing custody of Marco to the boy's real father. That was the reason

Effing's obituaries are sent off.

Solomon Barber replies and goes to NYC.

Solomon's appearance

Solomon's life story:

– his relationship with Emily Fogg

why Victor and Marco moved from Chicago to St. Paul, Minnesota for some years.

Solomon Barber has been obese since his youth, when he started to overeat. Obesity became a form of self-inflicted injury to his body. His huge size and weight made him an outsider early on, as people would stare at him and make fun of him. He sought refuge in books and spiritual matters, where he could forget about his body. He was a brilliant student, went to Columbia University in 1936, and continued his history studies in Graduate School. He was turned down by the army due to his weight. Instead he finished his thesis on Bishop Berkeley and the Indians in 1944 and started teaching at a college in Ohio. After his dismissal from the college he no longer cared about what happened to his body. He lost his hair and shaved off what was left. He began to wear various hats to cover his enormous bald head, and became known as "*the Man Who Wore Hats*" (p.241, l.42). He took up teaching again at various minor Midwestern colleges, where he was well-liked by his students and admired for his intellectual brilliance and teaching abilities. He wrote books and articles on early American history and Indians which won academic praise, yet he never managed to get a teaching job at more renowned colleges. A further hindrance to his academic career were his left-wing activities during his student days (he had been involved in the peace movement in the 1930s). During the period of anti-communist suspicion (led by Senator McCarthy) in the late 1940s and early 1950s these were regarded as reason enough to deny him better academic positions. So he continued a life of relative unimportance devoted to teaching and writing.

– his obesity

– his studies

– his hats

– his career as a teacher

– the books he writes

From what Marco and Barber can reconstruct later on when they tell each other their life stories, it is possible that Uncle Victor and Barber encountered each other several times: at the New York World's Fair in 1939 (even Effing could have been there on his return from Europe); in Cleveland in 1946, when Victor saw a huge man in a restaurant stuffing himself with food; and when Barber replied to an announcement for clarinet lessons given by Victor. Barber's attempt to find Victor is the reason why Victor and Marco left Saint Paul in such a hurry in 1959. Marco is disappointed that he lost the chance of finding his father.

– Solomon and Victor's possible encounters

Barber does not tell Marco right away that he suspects him to be his son because he does not want to scare him off with the idea that such an obese man could be his father. He is afraid that Marco will consider him a madman and never talk to him again. What he does share with him on this first encounter is the story of his childhood. Marco and Barber share a fatherless childhood, but, unlike Marco, Barber at least knew who his father was. His family told him that his father had died out West before he was born, and that he was a successful painter devoted to landscape painting; many of his paintings were kept in the house along with other paintings by famous artists like Blakelock. Barber admired them and set up an exhibition of his father's paintings in the local town hall. His mother suffered from a nervous condition and was unable to bring him up properly, so he was raised by nurses and relatives and took to reading and writing at an early age. At the age of 17 he wrote a novel, *Kepler's Blood*, an odd story about the search for a lost father, based on what he knew of his own father. Indians, moon

– the absence of Solomon's father

– *Kepler's Blood*

men and humans figure in the story, which contains elements of science fiction, history and psychological drama. He later gives the novel to Marco, who enjoys reading it because *"I felt that I had a better idea of who Barber was, that I understood something about what had formed him"* (p.251, ll.52–53).

When Barber's mother died in 1939, he visited the house one last time and learned a little more about his mother from his Aunt Clara. She told him that his birth had caused his mother's mental instability, as he was an unusually big baby and she hadn't wanted to bring him into the world.

Barber and Marco take a great liking to each other. Some weeks later Barber returns to New York for a longer period, as he has taken leave from his college. The money he has inherited from Effing is not enough to live on for the rest of his life, but it enables him to take a break from college teaching for a few years. He asks Kitty and Marco to join him on a journey to Utah to look for his father's cave and the paintings. At first Marco has his doubts about the trip – the overweight Barber is in no condition to withstand the physical strain of such a journey – but in the end they decide to start on their expedition – without Kitty, however.

Solomon's and Marco's friendship

Solomon's plan to visit the West and search for his father's cave

Kitty has found out that she is pregnant and decides to have an abortion. Marco is desperate for her to keep the child. It would be Marco's chance *"to belong to something that was more than just myself"* (p.276, ll.14–15). Just like his own father and grandfather, Marco is now being denied fatherhood. Kitty argues that she is too young, that it would ruin her dancing career, and that it is not the right moment for her to become a mother. For Marco, on the other hand, the idea

Kitty's pregnancy and abortion

of becoming a father is all that matters; he feels that an abortion would be murder and would destroy his own life as well. He pays for the abortion, but their life together can never be the same again. Marco decides to leave Kitty.

Marco leaves Kitty.

Commentary

Solomon Barber's story is summarized

The story of Solomon Barber's life, which is the focus of this chapter, is told more or less chronologically, and not as Marco gets to know about it. Much of what Marco learns about Barber, especially concerning his birth and unhappy childhood, his relationship with Emily Fogg and his attempts to contact Uncle Victor, he hears from Barber much later in the hospital before he dies (Chapter Seven). Marco jumps ahead, summarizing and restructuring Barber's story, another story-within-a-story that resembles both Effing's and Marco's own stories.

the theme of fatherhood

The main theme of this chapter is **fatherhood**. Both Marco's and Barber's fathers were for a long time unaware that they had sons. Marco and Effing become connected through Solomon, the missing link in their lives. With Kitty's pregnancy, Marco's fatherhood comes within reach, yet it is denied to him by the abortion. On another level, Barber's novel *Kepler's Blood* addresses the theme of fatherhood in a sensational way full of pathos from the point of view of an adolescent who is suffering from the absence of his father.

We are already familiar with the way **names** can possess a variety of meanings (M.S. Fogg, Effing). "Solomon" also lends itself to different interpretations, most of which are explained in the novel:

the various meanings of the name "Solomon"

- the cosmic dimension: earth – sun – moon; all of these are contained in his first name: SOL = earth/sun – OMON = MOON. He believes that "*he alone was able to encompass all the contradictions of the universe*" (p.249, ll.40–41). His shaven head resembles an orbiting planet accompanying his body.
- the three o's in his name reflect his roundness.
- a homonym of "solitaire" and "Solly Tear" (cf. p.268, l.15): Aunt Clara used to call him Solly and she likes to play "solitaire", a game of cards for one person.

Barber's **physical appearance** contrasts strongly with both Marco's and Effing's. From a biological view Barber does not conform to the family line: "*a genetic mishap, a renegade seed that had run wild, blossoming beyond all measure*" (p.233, ll.51–52). It is Uncle Victor who points out the connection between eating too much and eating too little, between stuffing and starving (cf. p.244, ll.34–35). Barber's obesity developed in his youth, probably as an expression of his unhappiness concerning his family – an absent (or dead) father and an insane mother. He seems to be trapped in his huge body as if in a prison. His fatness provokes hurtful and humiliating remarks from other people, and he becomes more introspective and

Overeating (Solomon) and starving (Marco) are the opposite sides of the same coin.

Like Marco, Solomon isolates himself from others, which leads to introspection and the absorption of knowledge.

less outgoing. He studies, reads widely and develops an intellectual mindset. He eventually manages to achieve a kind of balance between inner and outer self, between mind and body. He knows that there is nothing he can do about his huge body, so he accepts it as an inevitable fact of his life and develops a more humorous and self-ironic attitude towards it. As he sticks out already, he makes his appearance all the more extravagant by wearing outlandish hats. Even his social isolation no longer bothers him any more, and he is satisfied with being a well-liked and admired teacher. When Marco meets him for the first time, his smile immediately wins him over. His friendliness and concern for his son make it easy for Marco to become fond of him.

Solomon's feelings of fatherhood contrast with those of Effing.

On realizing that he is Marco's **father**, he acts in a responsible and concerned way towards his son. Even the fact that he does not tell him outright that he believes Marco to be his son is due to fatherly concern: he is afraid that Marco won't accept him, and wants to give him more time to become accustomed to the thought of him being his father. The bond that develops between them results from similar intellectual and emotional dispositions. They share a fatherless childhood, an academic education at Columbia, a politically left-wing orientation, and a fondness for odd clothing. Both have been searching for their identities – a major psychological driving force in their lives.

An ideology concerning America was born with its discovery and evolved with its settlement.

Barber's academic interest in **early American history** may be connected to his "fatherless" identity: he does research on Bishop Berkeley, the lost colony of Roanoke, the American wilderness, as well as Thomas Harriot, an astronomer and explorer who participated in one of the settlement projects in Virginia and who began mapping the moon. Berkeley was the first person to connect the idea of westward movement towards America with the hope of bringing civilization and progress to the new continent (a forerunner of the idea of Manifest Destiny), leaving behind the old, tired and conservative societies of Europe. Berkeley was engaged in teaching Indians and bringing higher learning to the native population. Barber's quest into the past of his young and "rootless" country is also a search for an American identity, an attempt to define what America means to him.

The story of ***Kepler's Blood*** is a strange and confusing text set apart from the rest of the novel, another story-within-a-story, loosely connected to the theme of fatherhood. Just as with the other "inserted story" – the Gresham brothers' episode – the point is that literary quality does not really matter. Every text is equally valuable and may serve different purposes. *Kepler's Blood* is typical of the pubescent outpourings of personal misfortune and emotional setbacks. It also deals with many themes in *Moon Palace*: the search for a father, Indian myths and story-telling, contact between Europeans and Indians, rejection, guilt and expiation, the opening of the West, and the emergence of modern civilization. *Kepler's Blood* reveals the mind of a younger Barber. Just as Auster himself wrote texts of an inferior quality when he was younger, so too did Barber.

another story-within-a-story

The other important issue in this chapter is Marco's separation from Kitty, caused by her determination to have an **abortion**. As Marco has suffered from a fatherless childhood, it is understandable that he wants to see his child come into the world. His reaction to the pregnancy is egotistical: he never talks about the child itself

Marco's main concern is his own fatherhood.

and its future; he is only concerned with his own longing to be connected to a greater whole – his own family line. Kitty is quite rational about her pregnancy: she cannot pursue her dancing career with a baby, and she feels she is too young to be a mother. Their difference of opinion leads to the break-up. Looking back at that period, he regrets his selfishness and blames the break-up partly on their inability to manage the crisis. *"Perhaps if we had been more combative in our relations, if we had spent our time arguing and throwing dishes at each other, we might have been better prepared to handle the crisis"* (p.274, l.37 – p.275, l.39). As it is, their relationship is based less on communication than on erotic attraction. Once they have to cope with a crisis which demands argumentation, discussion and mutual understanding, they are not prepared for it and so their relationship fails.

Revision
(what you learn in this chapter)

- This chapter deals with the theme of lost fatherhood: Barber expresses his need for a father in his fictional work, *Kepler's Blood*; Marco finds his lost father, yet loses his child.
- Barber's interest in early American history reflects the search for identity on a larger scale.

Quotes	Analysis
I did not have the feeling that I had moved to another part of the town. I had traveled halfway around the world to get where I was, and it stood to reason that nothing should be familiar to me anymore, not even myself. (p. 228, ll. 16–19)	A new life starts for Marco in Chinatown where he feels a stranger and an outsider. However, this does not bother him in the least. Earlier on, he liked to play the role of an odd outsider, wearing odd clothes. This experience reminds the reader of Columbus thinking he had traveled to China instead of the Americas.
Anyone who eats like that is trying to kill himself. It's the same thing as watching a man starve to death. (p. 244, ll. 34–35)	Victor draws a parallel between Barber's and Marco's problems with eating: stuffing and starving are not opposing states but are just variations of a psychological problem.
It seemed right to him that the vast globe of his body should now have a moon to go with it. (p. 240, ll. 34–35)	This refers to Barber's enormous bald head. Once again the idea of the moon occurs.
The baby was my chance to undo the loneliness of my childhood, to be part of a family, to belong to something that was more than just myself. (p. 276, ll. 13–15)	Marco can only think of the baby in terms of genealogy: he wants his family line to extend, to continue.

Chapter Seven

Summary

Following his separation from Kitty, Marco has a physical and emotional breakdown. Fortunately, Solomon takes him in and cares for him in every possible way. Not only does he pay for Marco's expenses (nearly all the money he inherited from Effing's was spent paying for the abortion), he also tries to take his mind off his problems. Solomon even makes an unsuccessful attempt to reunite Kitty and Marco. Unable to get over the loss of Kitty, Marco is finally persuaded to accompany Solomon on his trip to find Effing's cave.

Marco moves in with Solomon.

They carefully plan their route and agree to take a detour to Chicago, where Marco wants to visit the cemetery where Uncle Victor and his mother are buried. They travel in a red 1965 Pontiac Bonneville which they bought second-hand for the occasion. Solomon is fond of the name, as Pontiac was the 19th-century Indian chief who fought against the white man. On the road they begin to talk about shared topics of interest and they compare their favorite things in various areas of life.

Solomon and Marco set off to find Effing's cave.

On arriving at the cemetery in Chicago, Marco notices that Solomon is becoming unusually quiet. At the graveside Solomon starts sobbing and talking about Emily. In this moment Marco suddenly understands that Solomon is his father. He is so shocked and angry that he hits him on the arm, calls him a liar and insults him; Solomon backs off, loses balance, and falls backward into a newly-dug grave, hurting himself badly.

At the cemetery Solomon reveals he is Marco's father.

Marco reacts violently and Solomon falls into a grave.

Solomon is pulled out of the grave with the help of a crane and taken to hospital. After four days in a coma, he regains consciousness. He is unable to move due to a broken back and fractured skull. Lying covered in plaster in a hospital bed, he tells Marco his story (which has mostly been recounted in Chapter Six). Marco spends his days sitting by his bed, listening to him.

Solomon's time in the hospital

Marco is reluctant to believe that Solomon is really his father. He considers the possibility that his mother might have had other lovers besides Solomon. However, as Solomon loses weight in bed and as his hair grows back, common facial traits shared by Marco and Solomon start to emerge, and the father starts to resemble his son. Marco can finally accept that Solomon is his father. The little time that remains for them before Solomon dies is spent telling each other the stories of their lives. Solomon dies on 4 September. Marco has the need to talk to someone about what has happened and calls Kitty. Kitty is very understanding, but is not interested in taking Marco back.

Solomon dies.

Solomon is buried next to Emily and Victor in the cemetery. Before he leaves the desolate motel room in which he has spent the last few weeks, Marco smashes up the furniture in a frenzy, which makes him feel better.

With nowhere else to go, he continues alone on their planned journey to the West, first to Nebraska, then Colorado and finally Utah, where he comes to understand what Effing had meant when he talked about the hugeness and emptiness of the landscape. He explores the countryside around the town of Bluff, and meets people who claim to remember the Gresham brothers, "*the last of the Wild West train robbers*" (p. 299, ll. 69f.).

Marco heads West alone.

Lake Powell and Rainbow Bridge

Marco discovers that the whole area has been flooded and turned into Lake Powell. He realizes that searching for the cave will be fruitless. He rents a boat and spends the day cruising on the lake; on his return he discovers that the Pontiac and most of his money have been stolen. Once again he is penniless. With only his knapsack, he starts walking. He sleeps in the open and walks all the way to the Pacific coast, which takes him about three months. At first he is full of anger, but gradually this gives way to a sense of happiness, as he realizes that he is now ready to start a new life, having at last found out who he really is.

Effing's cave is probably under Lake Powell.

Marco's car and money are stolen. He then walks until he reaches the Pacific Ocean.

Commentary

This last chapter is the shortest in the novel. It literally rushes to its ending, as the time span of several months is condensed into the last two pages. It binds the various lines of the plot into a complex network of personal and national history, but some questions remain open in the end.

The perspective is exclusively Marco's. Only at one point can we actually hear Solomon's voice, discussing the pros and cons of traveling West in a dialogue with Marco.

Although the reader already knows that Solomon is Marco's father, we now learn about the circumstances of this disclosure to Marco. The fall which kills Solomon happens accidently, yet one may ask who is to blame for it. Marco reacts violently at the grave when Solomon starts to cry, and some form of physical force is involved, e.g. pushing and shoving. Yet when Solomon stumbles backwards, he retreats by himself: "*his face was buried in his hands as he walked. Blind to everything around him.*" (p.288, ll.31–32). One may say that his blindness to the world around him is responsible for his fall. He could have told Marco much earlier what he most needed to know – that he is his father. Blindness is once again used as a metaphor for the failure to see behind the facade of things and discover the truth of the world. Marco's violent outburst and Solomon's blindness indicate guilt on both sides; both father and son try to make amends for it in the short time that remains.

Once again the question of guilt is raised.

In the aftermath of the fall we experience Solomon's physical transformation. As a consequence of his eating less in hospital, he starts to shrink. By losing his fat he becomes another person: he changes from a lonely outsider into a loving and caring father. It is only as the "reduced" version of Solomon emerges that Marco can truly accept him as a father. Only when Marco discovers their physical resemblance is he prepared to accept Solomon's fatherhood.

The fall into the grave leads to Solomon's transformation.

Marco becomes a loving son. As if to atone for his violent reaction at the grave, Marco cares for

Marco had also cared for Effing before he died. Solomon earlier looked after Marco (just as Zimmer had done).

Solomon day and night. He sits at his bedside and they talk to each other about their lives. After Solomon's death, Marco has him buried in the Jewish cemetery according to Jewish rituals, so that Solomon is accepted as a member of the Fogg family: "*the Fogg family plot still had room for one more person*" (p. 296, ll. 3–4). Marco's decision to continue the journey that they had planned together is a form of commemoration of both his grandfather and father.

Note the ambiguity of the word "plot" ("area in a grave-yard" and "story-line").

As Marco drives west in search of his grandfather's cave, he is conforming to the American tradition of the Westward quest. Effing's journey was to discover the openness and vastness of the landscape. While he did discover a creative intensity, he also emerged with a new identity born in theft and murder.

heading West in search of an identity

Solomon's experience of the West is of a more imaginary nature: his academic research into the beginnings of American civilization and his projects on the early colonization (Berkeley and Roanoke) trace the expansion of European settlement at the cost of older, indigenous civilizations.

Marco's trip is also an encounter with the past: he visits the ancient ruins of the vanished Anasazi, which grants him a new universal perspective, helping give him a new sense to his life. Emptiness no longer threatens him, and the idea that he will never find Effing's cave and paintings no longer bothers him. He had told Solomon right from the start of their expedition that the search for the cave would probably be futile: "*we would be left with nothing but the futility of our own ambitions. This was a metaphor I could live with, the leap into emptiness I had always dreamed of.*" (p. 284, ll. 4–6).

This reflects the life of the Indians in "Moonlight" (cf. p. 140, ll. 29–38).

Marco reaches the shores of the Pacific not by car but on foot. In a country where the use of cars seems to be a major means of survival, the decision to walk implies a protest against the dominance of technological advance. Yet being on the move seems to be a very American quality; for many Americans identity is often connected with the process of movement involved in immigration (to America) and migration (within America, e.g. to the West). Marco says at the end that he had found the answer to "*some important question*" (p. 301, l. 64), even though he did not know what the question was. We may conclude that it was the question of who he is. It is the journey, the process, the movement that count for him, not the result. The question as to what he will do next is not so relevant. Instead, Marco is reassured by the presence of the moon in its place in the darkness.

Revision
(what you learn in this chapter)

- Marco and Solomon set off on their journey to the West in search of the legacy of their father/grandfather.
- The visit to Emily Fogg's grave is a devastating emotional experience for both of them. Marco finally learns that Solomon is his father.
- Both father and son are partly guilty for the fall, Marco because of his violent physical reaction and Solomon for his "blindness".
- The transformation in the hospital finally convinces Marco that Solomon is really his biological father.
- With Marco's journey to the West the third generation re-enacts the two earlier ones of his father and grandfather.
- Reaching the shores of the Pacific on foot, Marco has left his old self behind and can start a new life.

Quotes	Analysis
If I had thought there was the slightest possibility of finding the cave, I doubt that I would have gone, but the idea of a useless quest, of setting out on a journey that was doomed to failure, appealed to my sense of things at that moment. We would search, but we would not find. (p.283, l.69 – p.284, l.3)	Marco is so desperate and hopeless that he falls back into his typical modes of behavior, which the reader is already familiar with from his time roaming the streets.
The story had begun without me, so to speak, and by the time I entered it myself, the action was already far advanced, the whole thing was flying out of control. (p.287, ll.51–53)	Standing in front of the graves, Marco is overpowered by his feelings. On recalling the scene later, he understands that it was really Solomon's story.
For twenty-four years, I had lived with an unanswerable question, and little by little I had come to embrace that enigma as the central fact about myself. (p.290, ll.36–38)	Marco is reluctant to accept Solomon as his father, because he has got so used to the idea of being an orphan that only the discovery of their physical similarity finally convinces him.
The hugeness and the emptiness of the land had begun to affect my sense of time. The present no longer seemed to bear any of the same consequences.[…] Of all the objects in the universe, nothing is smaller than the earth. (p.298, ll.32–38)	Effing had made similar experiences with the vastness and emptiness of the land. Marco seems to lose touch with the present and begins to understand intuitively the relativity of size, space and speed.

Once I reached the end of the continent, I felt that some important question would be resolved for me. I had no idea what that question was, but the answer had already been formed in my steps, and I had only to keep walking to know that I had left myself behind, that I was no longer the person I had once been. (p.301, ll.63–67)	Walking across the country for three months makes him forget the terrible things that have happened. It is the movement itself which counts for him. Reaching the Pacific coast is significant for Marco as China lies across this ocean. He is attached to China by his name Marco (Polo), by Kitty Wu and by the Chinese restaurant 'Moon Palace'. China has become part of his identity as well.
This is where I start, I said to myself, this is where my life begins (p.302, ll.5–6)	A similar sentence can be found on the first page of the novel (p.7, ll. 14-15), where Marco refers to "the beginning of his life" not meaning his biological birth. Now his identity is fully established as Solomon's son and Effing's grandson.

The Characters

When a story is told exclusively from the point of view of one character – as is the case with the first-person narrative of *Moon Palace* – the reader obviously gets to know this character fairly well, together with his thoughts and feelings, his perceptions and feelings about the other characters, and his views on the world. As for the other characters, the reader has to rely on the narrator's judgment and perception. The only way we as readers can really judge the other characters is when they speak directly (e.g. in a dialogue), but then again the narrator can choose to report only what he considers to be important or relevant for his story.

The advantage of a first-person narrator is that we can get a complex and in-depth insight into the narrator's actions and motivations, and can closely trace the steps of his development. In *Moon Palace* we get a close-up view of Marco's life and thoughts. Yet we are also given a vivid picture of Effing/Barber and Solomon Barber as well, as their stories are recounted in detail (and partly even in direct speech). Effing, Solomon and Marco as three generations of a family form a cyclical unit: that is to say, they share certain character traits and some parts of their stories, e.g. the westward journey, their transformations within closed spaces, seem to be repetitions of the former generation. All three of them are definitely round characters, as they develop in the during the course of the novel, their attitudes and judgments changing in response to their experiences. The other characters remain flat, not changing during the novel and representing no more than a single idea or quality.

Marco Stanley Fogg

His Physical Appearance

When we first encounter Marco in 1965 he is 18 years old and a freshman at Columbia University, but his story really begins when he decides to move into the apartment a year later. Judging by his outer appearance he is *"an oddball"* (p.22, l.9), *"a young man clearly out of step with the rest of the world"* (p.22, ll.6–7). Wearing Uncle Victor's suit distances him from his fellow students, and he even describes himself as they might see him: *"[the suit was] hanging on my skinny frame like some wrinkled afterthought, a sagging turmoil of wool"* (p.22, ll.27–28). The only other time we see Marco from the outside is when he sees himself in the mirror of the hash house on West 48th street. This is towards the end of his down-and-out period in Central Park, and he is in a desolate state. He cuts his hair with a razor and is appalled by his looks. *"My ears stuck out, my Adam's apple bulged, my head seemed no bigger than a child's. I'm starting to shrink, I said to myself, and suddenly I heard myself talking out loud to the face in the mirror."* (p.73, ll.57–59). Marco's physical transformation foreshadows that of his father, Solomon Barber, whose stay in hospital forces him to lose weight and to shrink, revealing his physical resemblance to his son.

His Imagination

As Marco develops in his childhood under the influence of Uncle Victor, he reveals a great fondness for inventing abstruse characters, places and names, for making up stories and for role-playing. He later gives a vivid example of this talent at the students' breakfast table when he tries to convince the others that men had already been going to the moon for a long time and provides them with fantastic stories of moon lore, many of which were gleaned from the many books he has read. Marco enjoys reading a lot, while movies have been a passion of his since childhood. Baseball is another of his pastimes, and Uncle Victor, himself a fan of the Chicago Cubs and later the New York Mets, willingly takes him to ballparks at an early age. Marco has also inherited a good sense of humor from Uncle Victor, which helps both of them overcome the hard knocks that life has in store for them. Although orphaned at the age of eleven when his mother was killed in a traffic accident, Marco seems to have had a relatively happy childhood with Uncle Victor, who provided him with as much emotional and spiritual support as he could.

His Philosophy of Life

Uncle Victor's sudden death in 1967 leaves Marco at a loss as to what do with his life and how to support himself. He experiences a form of physical and mental collapse. Overwhelmed by his situation, his reaction is one of total inaction. He drifts along without making any attempt to change his desolate situation. He seems to have a disposition to let things be (not too dissimilar from Uncle Victor, cf. p. 11, l. 54 – p. 12, l. 4), an unwillingness to interfere with the course of events. Indeed, he develops a whole philosophical system to justify for this passive way of life – "*a form of readiness*" (p. 7, l. 9) and "openness" for coincidences and chance events to determine the course of his life. As he tries to explain to the psychiatrist at the army physical: "*I thought that by abandoning myself to the chaos of the world, the world might ultimately reveal some secret harmony to me, some form or pattern that would help me to penetrate myself. The point was to accept things as they were, to drift along with the flow of the universe*" (p. 85, ll. 46–50). Even if he later comes to reject his former life, which resulted in his living as a tramp, Marco maintains his readiness for the unexpected and remains open for coincidental events to show him the patterns mapping out some form of inter-connectedness.

Marco the Writer

Marco is a writer struggling with language and the search for the right word. The fact that he is widely read helps him develop a feel for quality of a text, while the painful lessons that Effing teaches him about how to view and describe objects by discovering their essence are valuable lessons for him both as a writer and a thinker. He practices hard to describe the world to Effing with the appropriate words, and eventually comes to see this not only as an aesthetic exercise, but as a moral task: "*I was a monk seeking illumination, and Effing was my hair shirt, the whip I flayed myself with. […] The demands of words are too great for that; one meets with failure too often to exult in the occasional success*" (p. 125, l. 68 – p. 126, l. 3).

Kittty is fascinated by his literary efforts and calls him 'Mr. Writer'. She takes his writing seriously and encourages him, becoming in a way his muse. Yet it is interesting to note that their relationship is otherwise marked by an absence of language: their love is expressed through the sensuality and emotionality of body language, and when they finally separate, one of the reasons they cannot resolve their differences is because they have never learned to use language to argue: "*Perhaps if we had been more combative in our relations, if we had spent our time arguing and throwing dishes at each other, we might have been better prepared to handle the crisis*" (p. 274, l. 37 – p. 275, l. 39). In the end they no longer speak the same language.

Marco and His Search for Identity

What most shapes Marco's life is his search for identity. With very little to link him to "*something larger than myself*" (p. 8, l. 39), with no knowledge of his father and a mother who died early in his childhood, he clutches at any straw he can find to establish his identity. During his childhood his names "Marco", "Stanley", "Fogg" (as well as the many nicknames he is given) allow him to construct a frame of reference. Later it is Uncle Victor's suit – a symbol of his only family member – that "*was actually holding me together, that if I did not wear it my body would fly apart*" (p. 22, ll. 2–4). Uncle Victor's boxes of books contribute to his personal development, while binding him to his uncle; the last physical link he has to his uncle is a clarinet case, which he keeps with him throughout his ordeal in Central Park.

His need for a family emerges strikingly when Kitty gets pregnant and decides to have an abortion. When Kitty denies him fatherhood, he feels that she is denying him the opportunity to connect to a larger family network. Although he regrets his stubbornness later and is devastated by the separation from Kitty, he is unable to react differently.

Discovering who his real father is finally allows him to complete his own identity. Although the circumstances of this discovery – an argument at the grave of his mother which results in Barber's fall and injuries – are tragic, and the ensuing death of Solomon even more so, the revelation allows Marco to connect himself not just to a genealogy, but to narratives stretching back through his nation's history. While his Uncle Victor had supplied him with invented worlds of imagination and fantasy, his father connects him to the early history of the USA through the world of research, and his grandfather to the history of westward expansion and technological progress as he himself experienced it. Marco can now leave his old life behind. It is no coincidence that his story ends as he reaches the other side of his country and faces China. The process of constructing his identity has come to an end, and he can finally say: "*This is where I start, […] this is where my life begins*" (p. 302, ll. 5–6).

Marco's quest for identity is therefore not merely a personal quest. It takes place within the larger context of America and involves coming to terms with his country, its history and its present condition. Rootlessness and fatherlessness are not only coordinates of Marco's identity; they can be considered the determinants of an American identity. The process of immigration, symbolized in the novel by the change of the name Fogelman into Fog and then Fogg, involves a change of identity as well, in which the old European roots are left behind and a new American life and identity are created. Marco uses the image of a bird flying through the fog to express this: "*a giant bird flying across the ocean, not stopping until it reached America*" (p. 9, ll. 65–66). Both Effing's stories and Barber's research reveal the destruction that accompanied the westward movement of the frontier. Marco's failure to participate in another destructive enterprise, the Vietnam War, can be seen as non-participation in this particular manifestation of America's destiny. In the end Marco not only finds out who he is, but also what his country means for him.

Thomas Effing / Julian Barber

Different modes of presentation and points of view are used to depict Effing. Much of what we learn of Effing is naturally provided by Marco, who both criticizes him ("*he struck me as nothing more than a vicious old man, a burnt-out maniac living in the borderland between madness and death*", p. 111, ll. 43–45), praises him ("*a man I could even bring myself to admire*", p. 120, ll. 9–10), and even pities him ("*I began to see him as a tortured soul, as a man haunted by his past, struggling to hide some secret anguish that was devouring him from within*", p. 120, ll. 13–15). However, we are often given long passages of dialogue, in which we see something of his ill-tempered, surly, arrogant nature which is always redeemed by his black humor (cf. p. 130, l. 14 – p. 131, l. 55). Interestingly, half of his story is narrated in direct speech (pp. 142–163), with the second half being narrated by Marco in indirect speech (pp. 164–191). Obviously, the story as told in Effing's words contains sarcastic comments ("*Lovely, isn't it?*", p. 145, l. 45) or obscenities and insults ("*There you are again, the goddamned lightbulb*", p. 144, ll. 33–34; "*a pox on that frigid bitch*", p. 152, l. 21). His speech is true to the character as described by Marco, in that he is not only irascible, but also intelligent, pitying and rude, depending on what or who he is discussing.

The two sides of his character, that of the monster and that of the good man, are obvious right from the start. In the initial interview he takes pleasure in confusing Marco, e.g. by telling him not to jump to conclusions because of his eye-patches and by rudely saying Marco's name is a "*sissy name*" (p. 104, l. 12). Yet the man of deep understanding and the astute judge of character (p. 119, ll. 61–62) soon begins to emerge from behind his rude and impertinent façade, as evidenced the sympathy he expresses on hearing the story of Marco's mother, or when he gives money to the destitute Tesla, feeding the birds (p. 149, l. 49 – p. 150, l. 9). The monster emerges again when he kills the three Gresham brothers in cold blood and takes the stolen money, but at the end of his life he feels remorse for this, and distributes money to anonymous strangers as a form of atonement. Effing is well aware of how he is perceived by others, but he uses his traits as strategies to improve Marco's knowledge, skills and own qualities. At the end of the interview he warns him: "*If I take you on, Fogg, you'll probably grow to hate me. Just remember that it's all for your own good. There's a hidden purpose to everything I do, and it's not for you to judge.*" (p. 108, ll. 4–6).

Changing from one trait of his character to the other, undergoing the transformation from an unpleasant to a sympathetic old man, involves a physical change as well. At one moment he conveys the impression of being half-dead, and the next he becomes very lively and energetic. Not only does his voice gain "*surprising force*"; his whole appearance is transformed: "*He was no longer the comatose semi-corpse lost in twilight reverie; he had become all sinew and attention, a seething little mass of resurrected strength. As I eventually learned, this was the real Effing, if real is a word that can be used in talking about him.*" (p. 104, ll. 22–26).

The confusing tricks he likes to play are a way of demonstrating his power over others and testing them. When he claims to have caused the New York blackout in 1965 by the power of telekinesis (p. 107, ll. 45–56), his intention is to prove the power of thought over the inanimate world. When he walks around in the rain with his broken umbrella, pretending it is raining, he calls this "*[the victory] of mind over matter*" (p. 212, l. 31). His last triumph is the correct prediction of the exact date of his own death.

The purpose behind these strategies is to confuse Marco and so force him to question what he sees: he is not to accept the apparent, the obvious, but should discover the essence of things. "*Never take anything for granted*" (p. 114, ll. 8–9) is the lesson he wants Marco to learn. Effing becomes Marco's "*self-appointed mentor to my inner progress*" (p. 110, l. 38), a kind of spiritual (grand-)father who not only teaches him to see properly but also to put what he sees into words. He is a severe and impatient teacher who is hard to satisfy. The old half-blind man opens Marco's eyes and teaches him to see properly, a skill he himself learned during his time in the Utah desert. This skill is the first step towards becoming an artist.

Like the two other main characters, his identity undergoes a transformation, but in his case this also involves a change of name and personal identity – from Julian Barber to Thomas Effing:

- At first he takes and wears the dead man's clothes (a leitmotif in the novel).
- From George Ugly Mouth he learns details of the dead man's life including his name – Tom.
- The injury he sustains in San Francisco can be seen as a punishment for his crimes. Thomas Effing is now a man who is aware of his guilt and ready to take responsibility (giving money to anonymous strangers is another indication of this).
- Before he dies he accepts his fatherhood: one of the obituaries (the long version) is sent to his son Solomon, who now learns for the first time who his father really was.

All in all Effing is a contradictory character with vicious and mean traits, but also worthy of sympathy for his understanding of human nature and admirable for his brilliant intellect.

Solomon Barber

His most outstanding feature is his obesity, which to a certain extent mirrors the history and tragedy of his life. A big baby at his birth, he was apparently the cause of his mother's mental instability. He grew up without a father and with a mother who was mentally absent, and he made up for his emotional neglect by chronically overeating. Later he developed into a lonely outsider given to weird fantasies, but he was also a brilliant student at school, and later in college.

While at first he identified his body with a dungeon or a prison and suffered from the negative reactions of other people, he later achieved a certain balance between his body and his mind, even developing a flamboyant eccentricity as *"the man who wore hats"* (p. 241, l. 42). Yet he always remains socially isolated, especially after the incident with Emily Fogg.

There is obviously a connection between Solomon's obesity and Marco's experience of hunger, as both are diametric expressions of an obsession with food. In the novel, eating disorders represent an attempt to compensate for family loss. It is worth noting that Solomon begins his shrinking process the moment he admits his fatherhood. For him as well as for Marco the important *"link to something larger than myself"* (p. 8, l. 39) is finally established.

Solomon's name, like that of other characters, offers a variety of associations that are explicitly mentioned in the text, a technique of postmodern literature called "over-determination". Solomon is shortened to Sol, which could mean not just "sun" but also "earth". He is called "Solly" by his aunt Clara, who loves to play the card game "solitaire", so another play on his name becomes "Solly" and "Tear", echoing his loneliness and sadness. One could also point to the graphic presence of the three O's in his name, thereby mirroring the roundness of his body.

It is as a loving and caring father that Solomon develops his most sympathetic side. He probably suspects at their first meeting that he is Marco's father. Although he only shares this with Marco at the end, he always acts like a father towards him. He moves to New York on a pretext, to be close to him; he tries to save Marco's and Kitty's relationship; he takes Marco in and cares for him after the split with Kitty; he suggests the trip out West to look for their lost heritage. The relationship between father and son is at its closest in the hospital just before his death. Solomon is able to provide an identity for Marco, an identity that goes beyond the mere biological relationship. Their relationship comprises a deep mutual understanding, a sharing of life stories and historic interests, of experiences and preferences. In the end both have managed to link their identities to a larger context.

Revision (what you learn about Marco, Effing and Solomon Barber)

- Marco, Effing and Solomon Barber are the only round characters in the sense that they develop in the course of the action, and their attitudes and judgments change in response to their experiences.
- All three main characters are denied fatherhood.
- Marco likes to take on different roles for himself, and he has a fondness for inventing and telling stories.
- Marco tends to allow his life to be determined by chance; during his down-and-out period he refuses to take any action to improve his situation.
- Marco's long search for an identity only comes to an end when he discovers who his father is.
- Effing is an ambivalent character who displays the traits of a monster as well as of a good man.
- Effing believes in mind over matter and likes to mastermind his own life.
- Solomon's obesity is external expression of his sad and lonely life.
- Solomon knew much earlier than Marco that he was his father. His guilt lies in having kept silent about it towards Marco.

Vocabulary

Here are some vocabulary items you can use when talking about the characters.

Marco
- orphan, deep attachment to sb.
- play roles, use disguises, oddball,
- intellectual, intelligent, widely read
- existential crisis, tendency to procrastinate, philosophize, drift along
- connect to sth. larger than yourself, a link to sth. larger than yourself, search/quest for an identity
- openness, ready for anything, let chance dictate your life

Effing
- complex character, manifold facets, ambiguous, contradictory, unreliable, eccentric
- half-blind, invalid, frail
- vitality, energetic, strong will
- mentor, teach sb. to see beyond the surface of things
- sharp wit, black humor, sarcastic
- egocentric, irascible, bad-tempered, cantankerous, disagreeable, ill-tempered, irritable, rude, insulting, querulous, snappy, surly, testy, subject to whims and moods
- sympathetic, have a deep understanding, widely read, feel remorse about sth., repent, atone for sth.

Solomon Barber
- obese, overweight, suffer from an eating disorder, stuff yourself with food, protection against the outside world, unusual appearance
- intellectual, do research on …, expert in the subject/field of …, extremely knowledgeable, academic brilliance
- teach at second-rate colleges, publish articles, popular with students
- warm-hearted, friendly, generous

Kitty Wu

In contrast to the three male characters, Kitty fails to meet the criteria for a round character. She remains one-dimensional – as her character is based on a single idea or quality and she does not develop or change in the course of the novel. Kitty exists only in relation to Marco: she is his "*twin sister*" (p. 42, l. 38), "*a shadow-woman incubated in the darkness of my dream*" (p. 76, ll. 27–28); later she becomes the muse who inspires his writing; and in the end she fails to become the mother of his child. Yet her emotional impact on Marco is immense and the break-up of their relationship is a devastating experience for him. We never get to know how she really feels about Marco, or what the end of their relationship means for her. Kitty rarely speaks directly; even the lengthy argument they have about the abortion of their child is given in reported speech only (p. 275, l. 43 – p. 276, l. 31). So the reader is provided only with Marco's view of Kitty. Even her past is recounted by Zimmer, while Marco adds his own remarks to the tale.

Kitty Wu plays a decisive role in the story, as she takes the initiative to search for Marco. She kisses Marco first (quite unexpectedly), and when she becomes pregnant, it is again Kitty who takes the decision to abort the child and thereby causes their separation. At decisive turning points in Marco's life it is Kitty who determines the outcome. It is significant that immediately before and after the relationship with Kitty, Marco needs to be cared for (first, by Zimmer and then by Barber). Her strong will and character are reflected in various episodes: the fact that she does not budge from her decision to have an abortion, her determination to pursue her career, and her refusal to take Marco back.

Her Chinese background is part of the myriad references to China in *Moon Palace* (even the name of the novel is "Chinese"): the Chinese restaurant, Marco's name (Marco Polo, the first European visitor to China), and Marco's arrival at the Pacific coast straight across from China. Kitty's biography follows the typical pattern of immigration, whereby different cultures meet and sometimes clash – a confrontation that has shaped and defined the American identity. But Marco also mistakes her for the Indian Pocahontas when he is hallucinating, an indication that Marco is starting his new life (just as the first European was saved by the first Indian whose name is known to posterity, thereby starting a new life for Europeans in America). Marco repeats Columbus's mistake of confusing America for China, only here it is vice versa. The reference to Pocahontas is the first of many to Indians, whose history is not merely a record of their slow destruction by the white man, but also an example of how they too were capable of destroying their own civilization (e.g. the ruins of the Anasazi people in Mesa Verde).

Uncle Victor

Uncle Victor only appears in the first chapter of the novel, although he later figures in unusual reconstructions, for example when Marco discovers that parts of his childhood were influenced by Victor's fear of losing custody of Marco to Solomon, and figures out the various occasions on which Solomon and Victor may indeed have encountered each other (cf. pp. 243–247).

Victor Fogg is a lovably quirky character, who is devoted to his nephew. He makes a strong impression on Marco, shaping his habits and preferences (for baseball and movies) and nurturing his disposition for aimlessness and reverie, but also for storytelling and the exercise of his imagination. He is a musician given to dreaming and drifting along. In the end he has to face the fact that he has not achieved success in his life. While he is unable to leave Marco any money, he does leave him his books, which have a spiritual value, and his suit, which Marco keeps and wears as kind of protective armor until it is ruined.

David Zimmer

Marco's only real friend from Columbia is introduced into the novel by his absence: Marco fails to find him. He searches for him and finds Kitty instead at the breakfast party. Zimmer, on the other hand, succeeds in finding Marco in Central Park. Selflessly, he takes care of Marco financially, physically and morally. This also includes some making critical remarks concerning Marco's behavior, as he accuses him of acting irresponsibly. It is he who opens Marco's eyes to Kitty Wu's love.

Zimmer's literary career and interest are similar to Marco's and also to Auster's for that matter: a writer of essays and poetry, he is interested in French literature and works on several translations from French. He participates in the Columbus campus riots of 1968, is arrested and considers himself a follower of the leftist movement: *"rattling on about Trotsky, Mao and the theory of permanent revolution. [...] he resolved the dilemmas of human existence"* (p. 100, ll. 21–27) and seems to be more politically committed than Marco.

Zimmer disappears from the novel completely after that. Only an accidental meeting in the streets some 13 years later reminds Marco of the past: *"seeing Zimmer like that stirred up an entire world of forgotten things for me"* (p. 108, ll. 25–26) and he claims that the idea *"to write this book first came to me after that meeting"* (p. 108, ll. 34–35). The way he describes this meeting with Zimmer is not without a trace of malice: he has become a family man, put on weight and doesn't write poetry any more – the mediocre academic career of a once-promising young intellectual.

Mrs. Hume

Effing's nurse and housekeeper, Rita Hume is a minor character, but she is important for Marco as she is an ally when dealing with Effing. She has been with him for nine years and knows how to deal with his vicious behavior and disgusting manners. She even sees the vulnerable and pitiful man behind the mask of rudeness and despotic behavior, for example when she advises Marco not to be put off if *"he acts a little strange. He often gets carried away, but it doesn't really mean anything. He's had a rough time of it these past few weeks"* (p. 103, ll. 39–41). In one scene (when he plans to distribute the money) she speaks to Effing in such a strident tone that at the end of their argument Effing apologizes (p. 201, ll. 45–54). There seems to be a kind of mutual understanding and dependence between Effing and Mrs Hume, and she honestly mourns for him when he dies.

Mrs Hume's brother, Charlie Bacon, also has a small role in that we see the traumatic effect that working on the H-bomb has on people. He had a mental breakdown and is confined to a veterans' hospital.

Elizabeth Wheeler

Solomon's mother and Julian Barber's wife does not get much attention neither from the author nor from her husband. Her unwillingness to gratify her husband's sexual desires fits with conventional conceptions of the puritanical morality of 19th-century women. The birth of her gigantic "monster-boy" results in her mental derangement, so that she remains in the background of Solomon's unhappy childhood memories.

Aunt Clara

A former vaudeville dancer looked down on by the rest of the family, she ends up inheriting the family mansion. She is given to drinking, and tells him much about his early childhood and other family stories.

Hattie Newcombe

She is the Barber family's black cook. She inherits the Barber family mansion. Solomon left it to her as she was Aunt Clara's best friend, thereby showing how friendship can transcend race and class and be found where one least expects it.

Orlando

Orlando is the only other black character in the novel. When spotted by Marco and Effing, he is walking along the street carrying an umbrella consisting only of the handle and the naked spokes. He pretends to be protected from rain that is not falling. He is a remarkable for his imaginative power of "*bringing nonexistent things to life, of persuading others to accept a world that was not really there*" (p. 209, ll. 42–44). His message could also serve as a motto for Marco, who believes in chance and coincidence as determining forces of our lives: "*If you're not ready for everything, you're not ready for anything*" (p. 209, l. 60).

Themes

The Moon

The title of the novel *Moon Palace* refers to the moon, as do its first and last sentences, indicating that it is a central concept in the novel. However, there are so many and varied references to the moon throughout the novel that a single and straightforward interpretation cannot be given. Its meaning goes well beyond that of a metaphor (representing a single idea) or even of a symbol (representing a larger and more open concept). The moon functions on different levels that can be roughly distinguished by their degree of abstraction:

... as a planet

This is the moon in its literal being as a celestial body. In this sense it appears at the end of the novel, where it *"had found its place in the darkness"* (p. 302, ll. 13–14), expressing movement but also belonging: like Marco, it travels large distances, yet it is reassuring to know where it belongs.

The "moon" also allows us to determine our position on earth: through the technique of triangulation we can locate our position on earth and relate any specific place to another one, by measuring its coordinates. *"A here exists only in relation to a there, not the other way around"* (p. 155, ll. 62–63).

A number of references are associated with the moon landing itself on 20 July, 1969, yet in rather ambivalent terms: Marco happens to watch the event on television in a bar with a couple of customers who laugh at the President's comment that this was *"the greatest event since the creation of man"* (p. 38, l. 27). The event is also scorned by Marco, as he describes it in terms of destruction and mutilation. What also comes to Marco's mind as he watches the event is the idea of distance and loneliness: *"since the day he was expelled from Paradise, Adam had never been this far from home"* (p. 38, ll. 30–31). For all the progress and technological advancement that this conquest of space – referred to by President Kennedy as "the last frontier" – may embody, the moon landing also implies waste: the ticker-tape parade in the streets of

Manhattan for the returning astronauts is memorable for its 300 tons of trash (p. 48, ll. 2–4). Later on, Marco's landlord, Fernandez, comments on the pictures of Woodstock with ten thousands of people doing "*strange things*" by saying that their 'craziness' should be blamed on the space programs: "*You can't fuck with the sky and expect nothing to happen*" (p. 53, l. 47). That the name of the officer who informs Marco of the death of Uncle Victor should be the same as the astronaut's name, Armstrong, is one of those coincidences that Marco likes to see as an omen bearing some deeper meaning.

... as an oracle determining our fate

The moon is one of the most ancient oracles known to mankind. It is invariably identified with a female goddess, and is believed to possess powers of influence, divination and structure over human affairs as well as over tides and other natural cycles. When Auster uses the moon's symbolic relevance in terms of "fate" and the future, he is tapping one of the most ancient and potent symbols in mankind's history.

The fortune cookie that Marco opens on the last night before he starts his job with Effing, when Zimmer and Kitty join him at the Moon Palace restaurant, reads: "*The sun is the past, the earth is the present, the moon is the future*" (p. 100, ll. 32–33). At the time it makes no sense to him, but he keeps it, and when he discovers later that it is a quotation from Tesla's writings – about whom he learns later – it seems to confirm the "*weird and premonitory truth*" (p. 100, l. 36) that it had promised. When we reach the end of the novel, we may be assured by the rising moon that Marco has found the beginning of his life: that there is, indeed, a future for him.

... as a sign

The neon sign of the Chinese restaurant Moon Palace, which Marco suddenly discovers with great joy from his rather drab and gloomy apartment, makes him feel at home, a feeling "*that helped me to warm up to the place and settle in*" (p. 23, ll. 49–50). He regards it as a "*message from the sky*", connecting the place to Uncle Victor and his "Moon Men" and confirming in his decision that "*I had come to the right place, that this small apartment was indeed where I was meant to live*" (p. 24, ll. 5– 7). Indeed the apartment with its boxes of books provides a refuge in which he first manages to find some inner balance and then slowly allows his philosophy of chance to develop.

The restaurant sign reoccurs for Marco at the end of his Central Park episode. In a state of delirium he has a vision of large pink and blue letters appearing before him. He sees himself hanging from one of the letters, obviously struggling for his life. Then the vision disappears and only two letters remain: *"The two* os *had turned into eyes, gigantic human eyes that were looking down on me with scorn and impatience. They kept on staring at me, and after a while I became convinced that they were the eyes of God"* (p. 76, ll. 1–4). This haunting image implies a sense of guilt.

... as a word

The word "moon" is also used as a pun: Solomon *"secretly loved it when the young girls mooned around him"* (p. 242, ll. 35–36), which takes up an earlier image – *"the vast globe of his body should now have a moon to go with it"* (p. 240, ll. 34–35) referring to Solomon Barber's planet-like roundness.

Other allusions to the moon include Uncle Victor's and Marco's admiration for the baseball player Wally Moon and his "moon-shot" home runs, and Victor's band "The Moon Men".

Auster also plays on the Latin word for moon – "Luna" – and the word derived from it – "lunacy". The mythological figure of Diana (the Greek Moon Goddess) stands for *"all that is dark within us"* (p. 38, l. 25), implying a state of mental disorder, of madness. Blakelock, the painter of the lost past, becomes a "lunatic" and ends his life in an asylum. Solomon's mother, Elizabeth Wheeler, becomes mentally unhinged, no longer able to care for her son. Marco himself is called a lunatic by a prostitute (p. 26, l. 9) after he buries Uncle Victor and feels he *"spun out of orbit"* (p. 26, l. 18), having lost everything that connects him to something larger than himself. He describes his state as *"a total eclipse [...] and darkness [that] gradually lured me in"* (p. 27, ll. 59–60) until in the end *"the moon would block the sun, and at that point I would vanish"* (p. 28, ll. 6–7). This is a description of self-annihilation. His later self-destructive experience in Central Park shows that he is indeed not very far from the state of 'lunacy'.

... as an object in art

In Blakelock's painting "Moonlight" the moon initially conveys a romantic sense of harmony and peace at first. It is only when Marco looks at other paintings of the moon by Blakelock in the Columbia Art Library that he discovers the similarity they all share: the moon seems to separate itself from its surroundings and change into something else, into "*holes in the canvas, apertures of whiteness looking out onto another world. Blakelock's eye, perhaps.*" (p. 142, ll. 21–23). The image of the moon as an eye is taken up again, but this time not as a haunting image like the "*eyes of God*" but as a nostalgic and poignant image, expressing man's longing for an irretrievable past: "*gazing down at things that were no longer there*" (p. 142, ll. 23–24). As such, the image of the moon goes beyond what one can see in reality, it transcends physical reality: it becomes "metaphysical" – expressing man's desire and longing for "*something larger than myself*", which can help us make sense of what happens on earth. In an interview Auster explains the role of the moon as "the longing for what is not, the unattainable, the human desire for transcendence" (from *The Red Notebook*). It is interesting to note that the fortune cookie sentence links the moon to the future, whereas the moon in the paintings refers to what is gone, to the past. Thus, the moon can comprise quite opposite meanings such as past and future, but then it also changes its shape constantly from full moon to new moon. The moon is inconstant and mutable.

...as a structural pattern

The beginning, middle and end of the novel are clearly marked by the presence of the moon. The notion of the waning and waxing of the moon, the cycles of growing and diminishing are repeated in other themes in the novel:

- loss and gain: Marco wins and loses money; he (like his father Solomon) loses and gains weight; Effing loses and wins wealth, he runs out of paint and canvas and discovers the walls of the cave can act as a substitute. All three men lose someone close to them, only to find someone closer: Marco loses Kitty and finds his father; Barber loses his father and finds his son; Effing loses Pavel Shum and gets to know his grandchild.

- food and hunger: Marco gorges himself on food at the students' breakfast; he nearly dies from hunger and malnutrition; Solomon stuffs himself since early childhood and becomes a *"fucking hippopotamus"* (p.288, l.27); Effing's disgusting soup-eating is merely a show he puts on.
- death and rebirth: Effing, Solomon and Marco's (unborn) baby die. However, new identities are created or discovered as well: Barber becomes Effing, Solomon becomes Marco's father (but is accepted as such only after losing weight and disclosing the physical resemblance to his son).
- destruction and construction: the surface of the moon is destroyed by the astronauts' flagpole while a new frontier in space is opened up; the 'golden spike' of the transcontinental railroad destroys the untouched wilderness of the west while it connects the distant parts of the country. The unbounded energy of the young American nation constantly destroys (Indians, Vietnam) while creating and progressing.

The cyclical repetition of themes and structures is an underlying pattern of the novel: three cycles of narratives (Marco, Effing, Solomon) are interwoven and connected through the themes of fatherhood and American history, but also through the reappearance of the moon at significant moments in the story.

Progress and Technology

Progress does not only serve the interests of mankind; it seems to always contain a malignant and destructive element as well. Knowledge of this is vital for Marco, as it allows him to shape his identity as someone who has learned to question what is seemingly good or seemingly bad.

The world of inventions and technological progress in all its ambivalence is epitomized by the figure of Nikolas Tesla. His career as a successful inventor and his ensuing downfall and financial ruin illustrate the sad truth that genius is not always rewarded. Moreover, his invention (alternating current) is seen to be ambivalent: it is, of course, on the one hand, beneficial for mankind, but it can also be used as a destructive force. It brings light into the world, but it can also be used to kill humans on the electric chair (cf. p. 145, ll. 44–45). Effing admires Tesla and seems to get some encouragement from him (cf. p. 148, ll. 2–8). He is fascinated by the inventions shown at the Columbian Exposition and the World's Fair. Yet when he meets Tesla again in 1939, he pities the old man, sarcastically calling him *"Mr. Tomorrow, the prophet of a new world!"* (p. 150, l. 1).

The most striking technological achievement of the 1960s was the moon landing. However, what is celebrated by some as *"the greatest event since the creation of man"* (p. 38, l. 27) is also ridiculed, denied, even considered dangerous, and is viewed by Marco as a form of mutilation.

Effing is cynical about the notion of progress. For him, progress means spiritual and aesthetic degradation: *"things move on, as they say. Progress. The bungalows and tract houses have taken over, every nitwit drives his own car. Hallelujah."* (p. 143, ll. 49–51).

When it comes to the destructive potential of nuclear energy, we see how it symbolically destroys Mrs. Hume's brother, Charlie Bacon. He refuses to fly the plane that dropped the atom bomb on Nagasaki by pretending to be crazy: *"Destruction on that scale is God's business. Men don't have the right to meddle in it."* (p. 223, ll. 41–42). Eventually he loses touch with the real world, and hallucinates haunting scenarios of hidden underground H-bombs sending out coded messages to confuse the Russians – another instance of lunacy in the novel. The cyclical nature of the novel is reflected in the fact that the Americans are once again in conflict with an Asian nation, this time Vietnam rather than Japan.

Chance and coincidence

Not all the events in the novel in which chance determines the outcome can be called believable. Examples include: Marco being found by Zimmer and Kitty in Central Park just at the last possible moment; the letter from the draft board being found the day before the date of the army physical; Marco finding both his father and grandfather merely by applying for a random job. Other examples of chance are more likely: the $10 bill that Marco finds when he is nearly broke; watching the same film *(Around the World in 80 Days)* he had seen with Uncle Victor. But in a work of fiction, of course, the author may stretch credibility, in order to serve the preeminent needs of story and message.

Marco is fond of omens, both good and bad, of secret messages from heaven, "*a prank of the gods, an act of divine malice*" (p.301, ll.41–42). He is convinced that there must be some driving force behind the events of our lives. Yet he never finds out what it is. There are many phrases like "*As chance would have it*", "*As it turned out in the end*" or "*Chance had taken me in the right direction*" in the novel. Marco is ready to accept that chance plays a major role in his life. This allows him to be receptive for anything that might happen to him, and to interpret any event as having meaning for his life. At the beginning of the novel he sums up the lesson that this experience has taught him: "*eventually I came to see that chance as a form of readiness, a way of saving myself through the minds of others*" (p.7, ll.8–10). While this may encourage him to find hidden meanings and to be open to life's quirks, it also means that he often passively waits for events to determine the course of his life. His total passivity in the face of financial difficulties result in his living as a tramp, interpreting small acts of luck as serious metaphysical events, and living so perilously close to the vagaries of nature that he almost dies in Central Park. Later, he admits that this was a mistake and feels guilty about it.

Auster himself has commented on the role of chance in his fiction. He has come to see chance as "part of reality" and claims that our lives are continually shaped by the forces of coincidence. He sees it as his moral obligation as a writer to incorporate the unexpected and unpredictable into his fiction. "Truth is stranger than fiction. What I am after, I suppose, is to write fiction as strange as the world I live in" *(The Red Notebook)*. All his novels explore this borderline reality and include elements of improbability.

Directly opposed to Marco's notion of chance and coincidence is Effing's belief in his ability to mastermind events, even down to the exact day of one's death: "*There are no coincidences*" (p.107, l.52). This determinism is just as radical as the passivity displayed by Marco during his homeless phase, and is equally in need of tempering in order to become viable as a model of life.

American History

Throughout the novel a large number of more or less famous names and events from the American past are mentioned. The reader is not expected to be familiar with them or even remember most of them. As an ensemble, they create a contextual framework of ideas and themes which emphasize certain aspects of American history (while leaving out others). A closer look at those names and events reveals a focus on the following themes:

Explorers and travelers: the names of Marco Polo and Stanley set the tone for the theme of searching, as they define Marco as someone who is searching for his identity.

Another group (e.g. Raleigh, Powell, Hayden, Lewis and Clark) are related to the exploration of Americas and the American west, the expansion of the frontier, the acquisition of virgin land. In a similar way, the astronaut Neil Armstrong takes possession of the moon – the last frontier. Other names like Little Big Horn, the Donner Party, and Lake Powell are names that resound with destruction and annihilation: they have left scars on the American psyche.

Victims: the Indians figure prominently here, being the main losers in the European colonization of the Americas. Men like Pontiac and Tecumseh represent a culture that has nearly been extinguished by the greed of the white man. *Moon Palace* continually pays homage to the indigenous inhabitants of the continent, even in a small detail like a car named after Pontiac: *"By driving this car out West, we'll be paying homage to the dead, commemorating the valiant warriors who rose up in defense of the land we stole from them."* (p. 284, ll. 36–38). Similarly, Anasazi, Roanoke and Croatan are names of peoples and places long lost; recalling their names and fates is a form of memorial.

Chroniclers: these are authors that Effing chooses for Marco to read aloud to him in preparation for writing his obituary, which is itself a kind of chronicle of a life story. The texts by Brendan, Manderville, Columbus and Thomas Harriot bear early witness to the spirit of adventure, colonization and civilization that characterizes the age of these explorers.

Artists: Seemingly the last ones to take stock of the process of exploration and westward expansion were the painters: on the one hand, we have the nostalgic mourning for a lost idyll in the paintings of Blakelock, who creates *"a death song for a vanished world"*; on the other hand there are the painters who celebrate the newly-explored and breathtaking landscapes of the West – Thomas Moran, Bierstadt, and Ryder. Their paintings gave the American public an image of the nature that America will finally subdue and assimilate.

Historians: Just as the early chroniclers retrace their steps into the unknown territories, so Solomon Barber, the historian, explores the early traces of the first colonies and colonizers. He is particularly interested in Bishop Berkeley, who was one of the first to use the ideology of civilization to encourage the settlement of the Americas. With its focus on early American history and the successes and failures of colonization, the extinction of cultures and the expansion of the white man's land, one can say that American history as presented in *Moon Palace* can also be regarded in terms of loss and gain, a theme which pervades the novel.

Structure and Style

Structure

The novel has a certain **symmetrical structure**: divided into seven chapters, the novel's middle chapter (Chapter Four) contains the description of the painting "Moonlight" with the moon as *"a small, perfectly round circle in the middle of the canvas"* (p. 142, ll. 17–18).

Within Marco's story lie embedded several other "stories-within-a story", all of which are interrelated through personal and thematic links. The most important links are those of Barber/Effing and Solomon, so that we can speak of **three cycles of life stories**: those of the grandfather, father and son. These life stories all revolve around the same themes ("fatherhood", "journey", "progress and destruction", "blindness and vision") and follow a repetitive pattern (isolation – fall – transformation – finding an identity). There are other shorter stories and episodes that to a certain extent can be considered **separate narrative units** as well, e. g. Uncle Victor's story, Kitty Wu's story, the episode of the Gresham Brothers, *Kepler's Blood*. The last two clearly vary in style from the rest, as they contain elements of pulp fiction (the Western genre) or adolescent scribbling (*Kepler's Blood*). This episodic structure, which consists of several interrelated stories within the ongoing story of Marco's life, emphasizes the fact that a person's own life story is not merely a record of that individual's life, but contains within it other stories and recollections, which become a part of one's life. Uncle Victor says: *"Every man is the author of his own life. […] The book you are writing is not yet finished. Therefore, it's a manuscript."* (p. 13, ll. 59–60). Only once everything has been put together to form a whole can one say that the book is finished. The stories of Effing, Barber and Kitty enable Marco to find out who he is, so that he can say at the end of the novel: *"This is where I start, I said to myself, this is where my life begins"* (p. 302, ll. 5–6). Similarly, the beginning of the novel contains the ending. Marco sums up his experiences and gives away the outcome. Seeing, describing, writing, painting, and narrating are all similar activities that involve the creative process of transforming life into a work of art.

Time

Marco's story begins in *"the summer than men first walked on the moon"* (p.7, l.1) – 1969. However, the actual course of action starts a little earlier, when Marco moves to New York in the fall of 1965. While the main line of action follows a chronological order, focusing on the years 1969 to 1972, there is a long flashback concerning Marco's upbringing with Uncle Victor, and detailed descriptions of the pasts of Effing and Barber. Throughout the novel there is a **continual movement between present and past**, which can make the time structure confusing for the reader.

We learn, for example, a lot about Effing's life as Julian Barber, particularly about the year 1893, when the eight-year-old Julian Barber, aged eight at the time, is impressed by Tesla's electric inventions at the Columbian Exposition in Chicago. The two years 1916–1917 are dealt with in detail, as the time in the desert and the cave are his formative years; on the other hand, the 40 years he spends in New York after leaving Paris are hardly dealt with at all.

What we learn about Solomon Barber's past is told in the opposite way from how Marco learns of it. The parts concerning his childhood, career and relationship with Emily Fogg – all of which are connected to the reason why Emily was so important for Barber – are introduced to the reader first, but are revealed to Marco at the end of his life when Barber is lying in hospital, while other parts of his childhood and the circumstances of his birth – all related to his father's absence – are described only towards the end of his narrative, but have already been revealed to Marco in the hotel on Barber's first trip to New York. *Kepler's Blood* is described between these two episodes (the meeting in the hotel and the hospital), but the book was only sent to Marco once Solomon returned from New York to Minnesota. So Solomon's story is described in exactly the opposite way from how Marco learns of it.

Marco's story formally ends when he reaches the shores of the Pacific Ocean on 6 January, 1972. However, his whole story is also told as a retrospective from the year 1982, when he bumps into Zimmer by chance and is surprised at his *"utterly conventional appearance"* (p.108, ll.20–21). Marco says that this moment was the initial spark that led him to write about the events of that time: *"I suspect that the idea to write this book first came to me after that meeting four years ago, at the precise moment when Zimmer vanished down the street and I lost sight of him again.*" (p. 108, ll. 34–36). Zimmer is wandering around like a tourist in New York, perhaps in search of his own memories. Aware of how different Zimmer has become, Marco decides to record the memories of the events that resulted in him "starting his life", so that he will not forget them.

The three life stories are related to specific moments in American history, with verifiable historical events like the moon landing, the New York blackout or the massacre at Wounded Knee creating a framework of real-life references in which the fictional stories are embedded. These references are not important in themselves but they convey the message that an individual identity is also shaped by its larger historical context. The history of exploration and destruction, of expansion and annihilation, of domination and oppression have all left their mark on the American psyche. The historical references are to be seen as reminders of the past, as witnesses of the guilt that is attached to the American processes of colonization, expansion and destruction.

Setting

The places and locations mentioned in the novel are not fictitious and most of them –Manhattan, Central Park, the landscapes of the West or the ballpark in Chicago – are well known to American readers either from personal experience or through the media, so that a few lines suffice to evoke an image of the place. Most of these places can be viewed as metaphors, as they suggest various states of mind, e.g. Manhattan street life, which forces people into a "*rigid protocol of behavior*" (p. 62, l. 16) or Marco's room ("*My apartment was bare now, but rather than discourage me as I had thought it would, this emptiness seemed to give me comfort. [...] Like an epileptic on the brink of a seizure, I had entered that strange half-world in which everything starts to shine, to give off a new and astonishing clarity.*"; p. 38, l. 33 – p. 39, l. 42).

But Effing points out the difference between experiencing a landscape in the flesh and seeing photographs of it: "*Everyone knows what those places look like now, you've seen them a hundred times yourself.*

Glen Canyon, Monument Valley, the Valley of the Gods. That's where they shoot all those cowboy-and-Indian movies, the goddamned Marlboro man gallops through there on television every night. But pictures don't tell you anything about it, Fogg. It's all too massive to be painted or drawn; even photographs can't get the feel of it." (p. 158, ll. 31–38). Places only become real when they are personally experienced. As a writer of fiction, Auster is not merely describing Manhattan, Central Park or the West but is giving them a meaning within Marco's life story. The painters of the West similarly created their own image of the West.

It is worth noting that Auster provides very few descriptions of the settings, whether they are apartments or landscapes. The settings merely reflect the state of mind of the characters.

Narration

As Marco is the protagonist as well as the first-person narrator, he is our only witness to the events that he tells: his perspective is therefore limited and highly subjective, but, on the other hand, the reader gains insight into his thoughts and feelings. It is important to remember when reading a post-modern novel like *Moon Palace* that Marco is part of a fictional world invented by an author. The author uses his own narrative to show the deficiencies of memory and story-telling. Very often Marco says that he cannot recall certain things, but other things he can recall in detail. One example is the altercation at the grave with Solomon, when he says he is initially unaware of Solomon due to his own grief ("*Whenever I look for Barber, however, I am unable to bring him into the picture*", p. 287, ll. 48–49; "*I can't recall the exact words*", p. 287, l. 60–61), yet moments later he records Barber's exact words and how the scuffle developed. Another example is the army physical: Marco says "*Much of what followed is lost to me now. Bits and pieces remain, but nothing that adds up to a full-fledged memory, nothing that I can talk about with conviction*" (p. 81, ll. 55–57). Indeed there are bits that he does not remember, e.g. what the sergeant said, what the other young men's feet looked like, how he got from one room to another. The unusual thing is that Marco draws attention to these memory deficiencies (which one might consider unimportant), before describing in detail the interview with the psychiatrist (p. 83, ll. 49ff.). Of course, it is more implausible that Marco remembers the exact words of a conversation than that he forgets minor details of the check-up. While indicating how unreliable the workings of memory can be, Auster is also drawing the reader's attention to the fact that the narrative is fictional.

Earlier in the narrative, the reader had been made aware of the thin line dividing fiction and fact, as Marco and Uncle Victor enjoy inventing *"imaginary worlds that overturned the laws of nature"* (p. 12, ll. 12–13). Marco first puts his narrative skills to use when he tells the story of Cyrano de Bergerac's journey to the moon as if it were real (p. 44, ll. 25ff.) – and this just after someone has declared that the real moon landing *"had never really happened"* (p. 44, l. 27). Here Marco is not interested in truth or non-truth, but in narration and the effect it has on the listener. When considering all the stories in *Moon Palace*, especially Effing's, it is always worth asking not "how truthful is this story?" but "how good is this story?"

This is particularly true of Effing's story, which allows for a whole variety of narrative modes. His general reliability is often questioned by Marco: *"So much of his character was built on falsehood and deception, it was nearly impossible to know when he was telling the truth."* (p. 104, l. 26–28). Indeed, even his present identity as Effing is a false one. His whole story in the desert of finding the cave, killing the Gresham brothers and finding their stolen money stretches the credulity of the reader, but nevertheless it is a good entertaining story. The reader is drawn into the story through the immediacy of direct speech in Chapter Four, as if one is sitting listening to a good storyteller. While the change to reported speech in Chapter Five is abrupt, nevertheless the tension and interest remain. Marco is showing that he has developed a fine narrative style, which is more objective than Effing's style, with its many outbursts and comments. As the story concerning Effing's new identity peters out, Effing and Marco are no longer gripped by his life story, and Effing starts inventing stories: *"There was no question that he was lying, but it struck me that he was doing it more from habit than from any intention to deceive me"* (p. 190, ll. 38ff.).

With Solomon's story there is no shift in perspective: everything is filtered through and adapted to Marco's point of view, even Solomon's novel *Kepler's Blood* is summarized and occasionally commented on by Marco himself (e.g. *"At this point, Barber's writing begins to stumble badly*", p. 256, l. 3). Unlike Effing's story, which is very much concerned with Effing's identity and experience, Solomon's story says at least as much about Marco as it does about Solomon. Auster has often been criticized for including Barber's juvenile writing, *Kepler's Blood* (p. 251f.), in *Moon Palace*, but it does have its place in the novel. This fantasy tale reveals an unhappy mind that is out of touch with the real world and is looking for solutions in a creative way. While Barber's story may be weird and unbelievable (and would never find a publisher), nevertheless it is included as an example of how one can harness creativity to deal with mental turmoil. Auster has included a bad story to display the thoughts of a troubled adolescent.

On a final note, the term "unreliable narrator" is often used in connection with the narration in *Moon Palace*. While the various story-tellers may be unreliable (and indeed the narrator often muses over his own reliability), the term is not really appropriate, as nobody is hiding anything, and the reader will not find a hidden truth behind the narration. Auster, in a typical post-modern way, is showing how an author can play with narration, and is revealing how memory is often unreliable.

Style

With its various narrative voices and range of subject matter (e.g. he description of a painting or a shoot-out scene in the Wild West), there are also constant changes in style. Descriptive passages alternate with dramatic dialogue and exposition (e.g. the explanation of technological inventions) with philosophical speculation (e.g. on the nature of chance and coincidence). The author adapts the tone and choice of words according to the particular situation. The most obvious change, as described above, is the shift from Effing's direct speech to indirect speech. This is not to say that the novel is just an accumulation of different styles. As a person learning to use language, Marco's style is very flexible and adaptable. It can incorporate all the different tones and voices required by the various episodes of his story.

When analyzing his own state of mind, he uses a matter-of-fact tone, which surprises the reader, as he seems detached from what he is describing – the psychological symptoms of his confusion. He does not bury himself in self-pity, but is able to examine himself objectively. *"I was trying to separate myself from my body, taking the long road around my dilemma by pretending it did not exist […]. In order to rise above my circumstances, I had to convince myself that I was no longer real, and the result was that all reality began to waver for me. Things that were not there would suddenly appear before my eyes"* (p. 36, ll. 37ff.). Looking back on his own life, he has become detached from the emotions and ideas that filled him at the time. This makes it easier for the reader to understand his motivation.

Characteristic of Auster's style is his use of approximation. This reflects his desire to show how memory works. He tends to avoid exact figures and rather speaks of *"two or three"*, *"fifteen or twenty times"*, he uses prefixes like *"mid-"* in front of *"month"* or *"term"* and *"half"* in words like *"half-read"*, *"half-world"* or *"half-literate"*. This also conveys the idea that the narrator wants to avoid fixed and definite statements. He also frequently uses paradoxes like *"he untaught himself the rules he had learned"* (p. 171, ll. 49–50), *"to see it is to make it vanish"* (p. 159, ll. 40–41) or Effing's rude remark: *"shut up and talk"* (p. 123, l. 66). Paradoxical statements like these reflect the need to avoid certainties in order to understand the world better.

On the whole, Auster's language and style are rather straightforward: he avoids elaborate vocabulary and figurative devices like metaphors or symbols. Only a small portion of the book is written in direct speech and talk, whereas reflective and descriptive passages are more common. Despite the complexity of plot and structure, the language serves the basic function of telling the story, or as Auster once said, "keeping things swift and lean".

Revision
(what you learn about structure and style in *Moon Palace*)

- Three cycles of life stories – grandfather, father, son – make up the novel, which revolve around the themes of fatherhood, journey, progress, blindness and vision, etc.
- Several other "stories-within-stories" are incorporated within the main narrative, which vary in style and tone.
- Story-writing is considered a process with an open end just as a life-story is never finished.
- Most of the novel follows a chronological order with the focus on the years 1969–1972. But a series of flashbacks as well as jumps ahead interrupt the chronological order of Marco's story.
- References to American history provide a factual framework for the otherwise purely fictional story.
- There are no detailed descriptions of settings. The reader is supposed to form an image in his or her mind.
- The first-person narrator has a limited perspective on events, but we gain a deep insight into the narrator's thoughts and feelings.
- Auster plays with narrative styles in order to show that it is the story and not the truthfulness of the story that matters.
- Auster's language is straightforward; he does not use many metaphors or symbols. He makes use of the technique of approximation and likes to use paradoxes.
- Auster adapts the style to suit different subject matters.

Vocabulary

Here are some vocabulary items you can use when talking about the structure and style.

- story-within-a-story, embedded story, cyclical narrative, chronological order, flashback
- limited perspective, blurred or deficient memory, draw blanks, bring sth. to mind, recall sth., improbable, coincidental, shift in the point-of-view, reliable/unreliable, out of touch with the real world
- in retrospect, interrelated, repetitive, frame of reference
- fictitious/real places, recollect an image of sth.,
- matter-of-fact tone, flow, change in tone, reflect/mirror a situation,
- elaborate, descriptive, reflective, figurative, be suggestive of sth.

Glossary of Literary Terms

ambivalence: the quality of having both good and bad sides.
character, flat: a character that has a limited number of traits or represents a single quality, and does not develop in the course of the action.
character, round: a character that usually changes in the course of the action, has more than just a single trait and tends to be life-like.
cyclical narrative: the repetition of themes and patterns within a group or sequence of stories.
flashback: a scene or an event that took place before the action in a novel or story.
(the) Western genre: a genre of literature (or movies, etc.) usually set in the late 19th-century West, in which there are standard events or descriptions like a gangsters, shoot-out, stolen money, etc.
figurative meaning: a word has a literal meaning (which takes a word at its face value) and a figurative meaning, which refers to another meaning beyond that of its immediate and basic message. The "moon", for example, in its literal sense is the planet, but it may have many more implications like "the future", "imagination", "love" or "madness". Figurative language includes images, metaphors and symbols.
metaphor: a figure of speech describing one thing in terms of another, so as to suggest some common quality shared by the two.
motif: a theme, an image or incident that is repeated significantly within a single work. It is sometimes also referred to as a *leitmotif*.
narrator: the voice of the person who tells the story in a novel and is part of the fictional world created by the author.
first-person narrator: a character in the story who refers to himself as "I". He has a limited point-of-view and does not know everything. He imposes his understanding and interpretation on the action. He can sometimes be "unreliable" in the sense that his memory is deficient or that he deliberately tells lies. With a first-person narrator the reader gains insight into the thoughts of the narrator.
third-person narrator: a third-person narrator is not a character in the story. He refers to the characters as "he", "she" or "they".

obituary: an article about somebody's life and achievements printed in a newspaper soon after they have died. Obituaries can vary in length and style.

postmodern: a mode of writing that questions the strict separation of high and low forms of culture. No one single universal truth is accepted. Post-modern writers tend to reflect on the writing process itself.

story-within-a-story (also: **"embedded" story**); a story that is told within the frame of another story. A story-within-a-story can vary greatly in length or style.

symbol: an object, word or phrase signifying something concrete that stands not only for itself but for an abstract idea.

Coping with Exam Papers

Generally, tasks on texts, whether they are fictional or non-fictional, fall into three categories: 1) **comprehension**, 2) **analysis** and 3) writing a **composition** or a **personal comment**.

1. Comprehension

All comprehension tasks aim at finding out whether you have **understood** the novel. Usually you are given an extract and are asked to locate it within the framework of the whole novel. You must select the relevant events which lead up to the extract and which take place afterwards. When answering comprehension questions you should refrain from stating your own opinion, unless expressly asked to do so.

2. Analysis

Analysis tasks go beyond a simple understanding of the text. You may be asked to deal with the whole novel or to deal with the selected extract in detail. Analysis questions often concern language and imagery, characters, or the way the plot is structured. Here again, you should avoid giving your own opinion. Be careful not to retell the story: you really need to analyze what is happening on a more abstract level, e.g. don't just say what a character does, but explain why he or she does it, or find an adjective to describe the character, etc.

3. Evaluation

This area covers a wide range of different tasks. Indeed you may be offered a choice of two tasks.

You may be asked to write a **composition** or a **comment**, which often require you to show that you have understood what the intention of the story is. Tasks often deal with a general interpretation of the novel so make sure your ideas are plausible and well argued. This means that your ideas have to be in line with the novel and that you must always be able to prove what you say by referring to the stories. Never just make a supposition and leave it at that.

You may be asked to write a "personal comment", which means you are obliged to give your own opinion, so make sure you base it on informed judgement, for which you need a thorough knowledge not just of the novel but also of the way it is constructed, so avoid making statements which you cannot prove.

Often you will be given the choice of doing a "creative task". Although at first this may seem easy, you should only choose to do a creative task if you have practised enough beforehand and your teacher seems happy with your work in this area. Creative tasks can involve:

- a change of perspective (i.e. recounting events or situations from the point of view of another character);
- reflection on other characters or events: this can often be in the form of a diary entry;
- filling in the gaps: here you might be asked to fill in what the reader does not learn directly from the text. This can often be in the form of a letter, an extra scene or an additional piece of dialogue.

Whatever kind of creative tasks are set, you must remember to stay within the context of *Moon Palace*. This means that you must not simply fantasize but look, for example, at the way a certain character behaves.

Operative Words

Regardless of which category of tasks you are dealing with, it is extremely important to read the task carefully and look for the operative words, which tell you exactly what is required of you. Here is a list of common operative words, in alphabetical order. (They are not necessarily confined to comprehension, analysis or composition)

Analyse ...: an analysis is a detailed examination of, for example, an important topic, the narrative technique, or one or more of the characters, so you must deal carefully with all the relevant aspects.

Assess ...: here, you must consider in a balanced way the points for and against something.

Comment on ...: here you are allowed to give your personal opinion on, say, narrative technique or the way characters behave, but you must always give evidence from the novel to support it.

Compare ...: you must highlight similarities and differences, most frequently between characters and events. A similar kind of task is:

Contrast ...: here, however, you should concentrate on the differences.

Describe ...: in this kind of task you must show what something (e.g. setting) or somebody (one or more of the characters) is like by giving a detailed account. Be careful not to forget any relevant details and choose examples from the text to illustrate the points you have made.

Discuss ...: if you are asked to discuss a particular aspect of the novel (e.g. its narrative technique or the characters and how they interact), you should examine the issue from all sides before you state your personal opinion.

Evaluate ...: here, you must form an opinion after carefully considering and presenting the advantages and disadvantages of a particular situation or course of action.

Examine ...: this is another way of asking you to **analyse** something.

Explain ...: this kind of task involves giving reasons for the action, characters' motives or how the specific use of certain techniques like the use of imagery or modes of description produce a certain effect.

Characterize/Describe somebody's character ...: here you should describe the specific features of, most often, one or more characters, by looking at how they are presented and the way they speak.

Illustrate ...: here, you have to make something clear by choosing relevant examples. Read the task carefully to find out whether you have to concentrate on the given passage or whether you may, or have to, refer to the whole novel.

Interpret ...: here you should deal with both form and content and how they work together to create meaning.

Justify ...: here you must argue why something should be done or some decision taken or why some conclusion was made.

Outline ...: an outline is a general account of something. In other words in your outline you can re-tell the major events of a story, or give a brief description of a character, which includes only the very relevant elements only and omits all details.

Point out ...: here, you must find and explain certain aspects of the text.

Present ...: here, you are expected to write something down in your words.

State ...: here, you are expected to specify clearly whatever is required. You may be required to state the main features of or development of something.

Summarize ...: a summary is more precise than an outline. When writing a summary you should select the key points and ideas etc. and structure them. As in an outline you should not go into detail or give examples. You might, for example, be asked to summarize a dialogue or argument, or the events of the whole novel or an extract.

General points to remember – or how to impress the examiner:

- You are not writing for yourself, but you are addressing the examiner(s) who will mark your work. Examiners are not mind-readers, so you must express yourself as clearly as possible.
- Always collect and organize your ideas before you start writing. In this way the examiner will be able to follow you more easily.
- When writing a composition or a personal comment, remember three simple steps: say what you are going to say – say it – sum up what you have said. Doing this will make your text more convincing.
- When you are dealing with literature you should always use the simple present tense when discussing characters and action.
- Structure your work by using "**connectives**" to link your ideas, so that the examiner can follow the presentation of your arguments. Otherwise he or she gets the impression that you are "rambling". You should be able to find a list of connectives in your coursebook.
- Likewise, avoid all forms of repetition, unless you want to return to a point you made earlier on. In this case you should use expressions like 'as I have already pointed out …'
- You can always impress the examiner by using suitable quotes, but they should only be used to **underline** a point you have already made or are going to make, and not instead of making a point – otherwise the examiner will think you are simply copying from the text or that you are unable to express yourself correctly. Always put your quotations in inverted commas. If you are allowed to use the book, you should also refer to the page and line of the quote.
- Usually the test paper will tell you how many words you have to write for each section of the test. If you have time after re-reading and checking your paper for coherence, mistakes, etc., try and count your words, as you may have marks deducted for writing too little or too much.

Written Test

At some stage while reading *Moon Palace* in class, you will have to do a written test. What the test looks like will to some extent depend on the *Bundesland* you are in.

Test

Paul Auster, *Moon Palace*
Excerpt from Chapter Four
p. 138, l. 26 – p. 141, l. 48.

Tasks

1. **Describe the effect of the painting on Marco.**
2. **Examine the steps Marco takes in the description of the painting.**
3. **Contrast Blakelock's vision of the West in "Moonlight" with other visions of the West presented in the novel.**

Dealing with the Test

The following are not to be considered model solutions, but hints and things for you to think about so that you can write your own answer.

1

Be careful not to retell the whole passage but only those items that relate to Marco's state.

You are asked to talk about the emotional impact which the visit to the museum has. First underline all the references to Marco's reaction like "I could not help feeling disappointed", "it confused me", "I was shocked to see", "I asked myself", "I wondered", etc.. so that you know at which point he "reacts". Verbs like "surprise", "puzzle", "disappoint", "admire", etc. will come in useful when describing Marco's reactions. Watch out for Marco's gradual recognition of what the painting may stand for: *"the more [...], the more [...]"*. These words indicate long and deep reflection.

When writing your answer, you could give a general description of the effect produced by the painting: you could point out that Marco's initial disappointment gives way to an admiration of the harmony expressed in the painting and finally to an understanding of its deeper meaning. Then you can deal with his reactions step-by-step: at first, he is surprised at the small size and absence of color, he is disappointed in Effing's choice because he would have expected a more dramatic scene. You might mention that he admires the professional quality of the painting but is shocked at the seemingly unnatural use of color. He is puzzled by the size of humans in relation to the landscape. Finally you should point out that Marco is disturbed by the discrepancy between the date of the painting and the idyllic world of the Indians, which was about to disappear.

2

Here you are to examine the overall structure of the description and the systematic order of Marco's observations. You might start with a general remark that Marco, when looking at the painting, follows Effing's advice not to stop at the surface of things. He gradually moves from observing the detail to speculating on the message of the painting. It may help to distinguish three steps:

1. The appearance: the size of the painting and its absence of color; the objects and how they are presented (located in different sections of the painting, following the movement of the eye).
2. The technique: He observes color and style; he compares his findings to reality. There is another point that should be considered in this context: Marco is puzzled by the greenish color of the sky as well as the size of the humans in relation to the immense sky.
3. The message: He is puzzled by the harmony of man within nature. He considers the discrepancy between what the painting depicts and what was happening at the time, and draws the conclusion that the painting must be a retrospective and nostalgic view.

3

When asked to contrast one thing with another, you must first briefly state what it is you should contrast. As the theme of the West occurs at many places in the novel in always different contexts and meanings, you must make a choice here and pick what you consider the most interesting and relevant "visions". Limit your choice to three or four examples and then outline them in relation to Blakelock's. First you should outline Blakelock's vision:

– Blakelock's vision of the west is a nostalgic one: he feels sorry for the loss of the harmony between the Indian and his world.

Here are some examples of other visions of the West in the novel:

– The painter Thomas Moran is the exact opposite of Blakelock and his vision of the west is that of the explorer who takes possession of the land in the west, presenting the newly-acquired and discovered majestic landscapes to the people of the East.
– The Gresham brothers' episode, which is presented as stereotypical Western literature, involving shooting, money and heavy drinking.
– Marco's own experiences in the West after Solomon's death. He is overwhelmed by the landscape and feels that he and the planet are insignificant.